Thinking Through Geography

Editor:

David Leat

University of Newcastle

Thinking Through Geography Team

Simon Chandler	The King Edward VI School, Northumberland (formerly Cramlington High School, Northumberland)
Liz Evans	Haydon Bridge High School, Northumberland (formerly Seaton Burn High School, North Tyneside)
Lynda Evans	Gosforth High School, Newcastle (formerly Walbottle School, Newcastle)
David Kinninment	Blyth Community College, Northumberland (formerly Blyth Tynedale High School, Northumberland)
Rachel Lofthouse	Newcastle University (formerly Prudhoe Community High School, Northumberland)
Julie McGrane	St Thomas More RC Comprehensive School, North Tyneside
Adam Nichols	Durham University (formerly Blyth Tynedale School)
Amber Riches	Formerly Harton School, South Tyneside
Deborah Smith	Walker School, Newcastle

Chris Kington Publishing

© David Leat
1998

ISBN 1 899857 99 0

First published 1998
Second Edition 2001
Reprinted 2002

27 Rathmore Road
Cambridge CB1 7AB

All rights reserved. No part of this publication may be reproduced, stored in a retrieval system or transmitted in any form or by any means, electronic, mechanical, photocopying, recording or otherwise without the prior written permission of the copyright owners. However, copyright permission is waived on those pages denoted as Resource Sheets which are expressly intended to be photocopied for multiple use in schools. These copies are not for re-sale or subsequent publication.

British Library cataloguing in publication data. A catalogue record for this book is available from the British Library.

Printed in the United Kingdom by York Publishing Services Ltd, 64 Hallfield Road, Layerthorpe, York YO31 7ZQ

Acknowledgements:

The following extracts are reproduced by kind permission of:

Ordnance Survey *Page 60*

Geography 14-18: Water and Rivers, Schools Council, and Reader's Digest *Pages 88–91*

Photographs of the Lynmouth flood *pages 90 and 91*: Tim Prosser.

Foundations of Geography: Waugh & Bushell, Stanley Thornes *Pages 100–101*

Contents

Table: The Exemplars: Topics and outcomes iii
THINKING THROUGH GEOGRAPHY
  Introduction 1
  Levels of use 2
  Using the exemplars 3
STRATEGY 1: ODD ONE OUT
  Rationale 9
Exemplar 1: River basins and flooding 10
  Resources *12*
Exemplar 2: Traffic management 14
  Resources *16*
Exemplar 3: Population and migration 18
  Resources *20*
  Adapting the strategy 22
  Afterthoughts 22
STRATEGY 2: LIVING GRAPHS
  Rationale 23
Exemplar 1: The demographic transition model 24
  Resources *26*
Exemplar 2: Daily energy consumption 28
  Resources *30*
Exemplar 3: The stage model of tourism 34
  Resources *36*
  Adapting the strategy 38
  Afterthoughts 38
STRATEGY 3: MIND MOVIES
  Rationale 39
Exemplar 1: The Kobe earthquake 40
  Resources *42*
Exemplar 2: A local nuclear power station disaster 43
  Resources *44*
Exemplar 3: Down and out in Sunderland? 45
  Adapting the strategy 46
  Afterthoughts 46
  Resources for Exemplar 3 . . . .*47*
STRATEGY 4: MYSTERIES
  Rationale 51
Exemplar 1: Industrial change in South Wales 52
  Resources *58*
Exemplar 2: Who is to blame for Sharpe Point flats? 63
  Resources *65*
Exemplar 3: The lost livestock of Loxley Coppice Farm 68
  Resources *71*
  Adapting the strategy 74
  Afterthoughts 74
STRATEGY 5: STORY-TELLING
  Rationale 77
Exemplar 1: Kingsley Osufu 78
  Resources *82*

Exemplar 2: The Lynmouth floods 85
  Resources *88*
Exemplar 3: The Nevado del Ruiz volcanic eruption 92
  Resources *95*
  Adapting the strategy 96
  Afterthoughts 96
STRATEGY 6: FACT OR OPINION?
  Rationale 97
Exemplar 1: The future of Antarctica 98
  Resources *100*
Exemplar 2: The Lost Angeles riots 102
  Resources *104*
Exemplar 3: Nature's number 106
  Resources *108*
  Adapting the strategy .112
  Afterthoughts 112
STRATEGY 7: CLASSIFICATION
  Rationale 113
  Resource Sheet, Thinking Skills (Introduction to Classification) *114*
Exemplar 1: The Great Kanto earthquake, Tokyo, 1923 116
  Resources *119*
Exemplar 2: The response to Hurricane Gloria, USA 122
  Resources *124*
Exemplar 3: Changing iron and steel location 126
  Resources *129*
  Adapting the strategy .134
  Afterthoughts 134
STRATEGY 8: READING PHOTOGRAPHS
  Rationale 135
Exemplar 1: Using photos to introduce geography 136
  Resources *140*
Exemplar 2: Urban land use models 144
  Resources *146*
Exemplar 3: The impact of tourism 149
  Resources *151*
  Adapting the strategy .155
  Afterthoughts 155
CURRICULUM DEVELOPMENT
Curriculum design principles 157
  1. Constructivism 157
  2. Metacognition 159
  3. Challenge 159
  4. Talk and groupwork 160
  5. Big concepts 161
  6. Bridging and transfer 162
  7. Appealing to all the senses 162
  8. Thinking skills plus .163
Long term infusion 163

The National Curriculum and GCSE 163	Planning 169
The National Curriculum 163	Decision making 169
Gifted and Talented, Citizenship and Creativity 164	Inequality 170
GCSE 164	Development 170
Graph to indicate thinking skills inputs,	**APPENDIX 2: PROFESSIONAL DEVELOPMENT**
processes and outcomes 166	Professional development 171
APPENDIX 1: BIG CONCEPTS	Professional learning communities 172
Cause and effect 167	Classroom Observation 172
Systems 168	
Classification 168	**REFERENCES** 175
Location 169	Further useful reading 176

THE GEOGRAPHICAL ASSOCIATION
GA AWARD RESULTS 1998

GOLD CERTIFICATE

THINKING THROUGH GEOGRAPHY

Thinking Through Geography is the result of a team of ten young teachers involved with the PGCE at Newcastle University. In its introduction it states that it is about "geography with a difference" and that the book was written to help teachers to move away from the overview that geography is a load of content to be delivered. It aims to assist teachers who do not want their pupils to be bored and demotivated, to encourage them to question and become independent learners. It is a book about professional development, introducing teachers to new strategies which require the practitioner to take risks in order to make the lessons more interesting.

All the strategies have been used in classrooms, undergoing thorough "road testing" in real life. The geographical content is high quality and appropriate to many teaching situations from Y7 to Y13 in a wide variety of schools. The trials are reported in detail to give guidelines to avoid predictable pitfalls to make teachers think about issues which will need to be addressed with the class. The latter part of the book encourages teachers to take the ideas further, both in developing their own strategies and in developing the learning of the pupils. There is some theory about learning and curriculum development to develop a "teaching thinking curriculum". It effectively combines geography and pedagogy adding to the professionalism of the practice of teaching.

The teaching approaches outlined are novel and a worthy addition to the geography teacher's repertoire. The resources are photocopiable and this is facilitated by the binding of the book and its black and white format. The exemplars have interesting titles such as "Mind Movies" and "Living Graphs" and the carefully prepared material will engage, stimulate and stretch students of all ages and abilities. Examples are wide ranging and up to date from around the world, addressing important "big concepts" in the teaching of geography and elsewhere.

The Geographical Association, 160 Solly Street,   Sheffield S1 4BF. Tel: Sheffield (0114) 296 0088
Chief Executive: M.R. Curry, LL.B   Fax: (0114) 296 7176   Email: ga@geography.org.uk
Registered Charity No. 313129

Table: The Exemplars

C = Concept developed through debriefing the exemplar (see page 167 for the concepts).
O = Other important learning outcome, relating to language, listening, writing, groupwork, etc.
National Curriculum (NC) Thinking Skills: IR = Information-processing; **R** = Reasoning;
En = Enquiry; **CT** = Creative Thinking; **Ev** = Evaluation.

Strategy	Topic and Year	Outcome	NC Thinking Skills
Odd One Out Exemplar 1	River basins and flooding Y7	C: Classification O: Developing vocabulary	IP, R, CT
Odd One Out Exemplar 2	Traffic management Y10	C: Classification Cause and effect O: Developing vocabulary	IP, R, CT
Odd One Out Exemplar 3	Population and migration Y9	C: Classification Cause and effect O: Developing vocabulary	IP, R, CT
Living Graphs Exemplar 1	The demographic transition model Y10	C: Cause and effect O: Using pupils' knowledge Speculating	IP, R, CT, Ev
Living Graphs Exemplar 2	Daily energy consumption Y7	C: Cause O: Using pupils' knowledge	IP, R, CT, Ev
Living Graphs Exemplar 3	The stage model of tourism Y9	C: Cause and effect O: Using pupils' knowledge	IP, R, CT, Ev
Mind Movies Exemplar 1	The Kobe earthquake Y9	O: Active listening Using pupils' knowledge Remembering	IP, CT
Mind Movies Exemplar 2	A local nuclear power station disaster Y8	C: Effects O: Active listening, speculating	IP, CT
Mind Movies Exemplar 3	Down and out in Sunderland? Y10	C: Effects O: Active listening Remembering	IP, CT
Mysteries Exemplar 1	Industrial change in South Wales Y8	C: Cause O: Group work Handling information Explaining	IP, R, En, CT, Ev
Mysteries Exemplar 2	Who is to blame for Sharpe Point flats? Y10	C: Cause O: Group work Handling information Explaining	IP, R, En, CT, Ev
Mysteries Exemplar 3	The lost livestock of Loxley Coppice Farm Y12	C: Cause and systems O: Group work Handling information	IP, R, En, CT, Ev

Strategy	Topic and Year	Outcome	NC Thinking Skills
Story-telling Exemplar 1	The story of Kingsley Osufu Y10	C: Cause and effect O: Active listening Speaking Remembering	IP, En CT, Ev:
Story-telling Exemplar 2	The Lynmouth floods Y12	C: Cause and effect O: Active listening Speaking Remembering	IP, En, CT, Ev
Story-telling Exemplar 3	The Nevado del Ruiz volcanic eruption Y9	C: Cause and effect O: Active listening Speaking Remembering	IP, En, CT, Ev
Fact or Opinion? Exemplar 1	The future of Antarctica Y12	C: Classification Decision making O: Handling data	IP, R, En, CT, Ev
Fact or Opinion? Exemplar 2	The Los Angeles riots Y8	C: Classification Decision making O: Handling data	IP, R, En, CT, Ev
Fact or Opinion? Exemplar 3	Nature's numbers Y12	C: Classification Decision making O: Handling data	IP, R, En, CT, Ev
Classification Exemplar 1	The great Kanto earthquake Y11	C: Classification and planning O: Handling information Explaining	IP, R, CT, Ev
Classification Exemplar 2	The response to Hurricane Gloria Y8 and 9	C: Classification Planning and development O: Handling information	IP, R, CT, Ev
Classification Exemplar 3	Changing iron and steel location Y9 and 11	C: Classification Cause O: Explaining	IP, R, CT, Ev
Reading Photographs Exemplar 1	Using photographs to introduce geography Y7	C: Classification O Visual scanning Geographical vocabulary	IP, R, En, CT, Ev
Reading Photographs Exemplar 2	Urban land use models Y10	C: Classification O: Visual scanning	IP, R, En, CT, Ev
Reading Photographs Exemplar 3	Impact of tourism Y12	C: Development O: Visual scanning Handling data	IP, R, En, CT, Ev

Thinking Through Geography

Introduction

This book is about geography with a difference. Geography is a brilliant, exciting subject—at least it should be. However, our main concern is not with geography, it is with children's learning and that is the difference. Geography is not an end or a thing in itself, it is a view of the world that changes as our knowledge and thinking changes. Its *raison d'être*, therefore, is not that it should be learned for its own sake, but rather that it should assist learning. The book is written to help teachers move away from statements like *'Pupils should be taught that...'*, away from the view that geography is a load of content to be delivered, and away from bland double-page spreads written to a formula that end with *'Why not investigate?'*. We want to assist teachers who:

- DO NOT want pupils to be bored and demotivated;
- DO want pupils to become independent learners who are excited by learning;
- DO want pupils to ask questions (even when we don't know the answer);
- DO want pupils to say things that make us say *'Hmm... I've never thought of that'*;
- DO want parents to come to parents' evening asking about lessons that their offspring have actually talked about at home.

Therefore this book is also about professional development because, as we have discovered, making these strategies work effectively requires you to take risks, develop your practice and learn more about students' learning.

Genesis

Many of these strategies started life with no theoretical basis at all. Some are original and some have been borrowed from other contexts, but they were developed to make lessons more interesting. They have all been used many times, some dozens of times and on occasions they have fallen flat, but generally most pupils really enjoy them. Most pupils do like being made to think, once they get used to the idea.

Over time, as we have thought and read more, we have realised that there is more to them than just making more interesting lessons, especially when we start to use debriefing. We have learned not only why they work, but also how to make better use of their potential for promoting learning. This has helped provide an antidote to the uniformity triggered by the National Curriculum (NC) Orders.

The **strategy exemplars** were all written up by classroom teachers, some experienced heads of department, others with a few years under their belts, and two in their first year of teaching! All had a close connection with Newcastle University Department of Education, all being ex-PGCE students or mentors in the teacher-training partnership. These teachers teach in a wide variety of contexts: 11-16s, 11-18s, 13-18s, disadvantaged catchments, more favoured catchments, Roman Catholic schools, inner city areas, suburbs, old mining communities and a new town. This says a great deal about the potential in the strategies for differentiation. It also can give you confidence that these strategies and materials DO WORK.

Levels of use

This book can be used at 4 different levels. The higher the level the greater is the potential impact on students' learning. But correlated with the level of use is an increased need to restructure practice—and that costs time and effort.

Level 1

You use the photocopiable materials as they are to create more interesting and challenging lessons.

Level 2

All the strategies are flexible and adaptable and can be used across a wide spectrum of ages and ability ranges. To demonstrate this, each strategy is exemplified by three contexts that range in subject matter and age range. Many of the exemplars can be used with equal success with Year 7 and A Level classes, with only the smallest of changes. (One *Mystery* concerning the Kobe earthquake, found in SCAA's (now QCA) KS3 *'Optional Tasks and Tests'* publication, has been used with Year 7 and Geography HMI.) Many teachers will be able to use the templates and adapt the strategies for other topics.

Level 3

To the above, you start to add **debriefing**. There are two main lines of questioning signified for this: (i) 'What is your answer/solution/outcome?', with supplementary questions to encourage pupils to be explicit, and encouragement to other pupils to comment, chip in and question; and (ii) 'How did you tackle the problem/How did you do it?' through which one gets pupils to talk about their thinking. Thinking and talking about thinking is termed **metacognition**. It is through this process that pupils start to gain an insight into thinking and learning, and build up an explicit understanding of **major concepts in geography** which can be **transferred** to other contexts. We freely acknowledge that debriefing is very hard to do well, especially at first, and can have the effect of making one feel like a novice again. At this level, professional development really becomes a very significant issue. Further guidance on debriefing can be found in *More Thinking Through Geography* and Leat & Kinninment (2000).

Level 4

Beyond Level 3, one is very definitely into the area of school policy relating to curriculum and staff development. If you want to make teaching thinking fully effective, it needs to be an approach to teaching which extends beyond just one department or faculty. There would need to be changes, for example, in policies and practice related to assessment, pupils' reading and writing, and an integrated whole school approach to the curriculum. This is demanding, but a growing number of schools are developing meaningful teaching and learning policies.

We have written this book primarily for those who are concerned with Levels 1 and 2. The strategies are presented to deal with those primary levels with some guidance on starting to address debriefing (Level 3). The last part of the book (pages 157–166) is aimed at those who wish to consider Levels 3 and 4 in more depth.

We make no apology for the appearance of some theory about learning and curriculum development. For too long teaching has drifted towards a utilitarian, delivery mentality. One of the dangers inherent in this is that it makes the profession very vulnerable to politicians, an imposed curriculum and OfSTED judgements. A **teaching thinking curriculum**, for example, allows you to resist the winds of political debate, because you know what works and why, and you can continue to steer this course, whilst adjusting to the external forces. We know that everyone is too busy, heavily burdened by too much paperwork, but understanding about learning has to be a priority for teachers, otherwise our claim to be professionals is hollow. We expect doctors to know a great deal about physiology, illness and treatments—teachers need to know about how to get students to learn.

To some extent the educational system has been following where *Thinking Through Geography* has lead. The Key Stage 3 Strategy includes geography in the Teaching and Learning in Foundation subjects (TLF) strand. This strand includes thinking skills. This reinforces the trend in the revised National Curriculum which requires all subjects to address the following thinking skills:

- *Information-processing skills*

    These enable pupils to locate and collect relevant information, to sort, classify, sequence, compare and contrast, and to analyse part/whole relationships.

- *Reasoning skills*

    These enable pupils to give reasons for opinions and actions, to draw inferences and make deductions, to use precise language to explain what they think, and to make judgements and decisions informed by reasons or evidence.

- *Enquiry skills*

    These enable pupils to ask relevant questions, to pose and define problems, to plan what to do and how to research, to predict outcomes and anticipate consequences, and to test conclusions and improve ideas.

- *Creative thinking skills*

    These enable pupils to generate and extend ideas, to suggest hypotheses, to apply imagination, and to look for alternative innovative outcomes.

- *Evaluation skills*

    These enable pupils to evaluate information, to judge the value of what they read, hear and do, to develop criteria for judging the value of their own and others' work or ideas, and to have confidence in their judgements.

From September 2001, TLF is in its national roll-out phase, requiring many more geography departments to engage with teaching thinking as a teaching style. In the pilot phase geography (and history) departments used TTG strategies to infuse thinking skills into their teaching and schemes of work, and took a lead in their schools in developing the teaching style. The roll-out provides further opportunities for go-ahead departments.

TLF will also offer training in managing curriculum innovation and coaching, which provide important building blocks in helping teachers move on to levels 3 and 4 in the use of these materials. Geographers should take the opportunities offered by TLF (which also include assessment for learning) to demonstrate the contribution they can make to developing pupils as intelligent, flexible and independent learners.

In the Table of exemplars on page iii the following key is used to indicate whether a particular strategy is likely to invoke one the skills described in the National Curriculum.

IP	**Information Processing**
R	**Reasoning**
En	**Enquiry**
CT	**Creative Thinking**
Ev	**Evaluation**

However it should be realised that there is a great deal more going on in pupils' minds and in the pupil groups when these strategies are used.

Using the Exemplars

Each strategy is demonstrated through three exemplars which were developed for and trialled with different age and ability classes. This demonstrates the inherent flexibility of each strategy, although the intentions and outcomes of using a particular strategy will vary with the age and ability of the class. For example using a mystery with a Y7 group is likely to contribute as much to intellectual development as it is learning content. Using a mystery with an A Level group, however, may focus more on developing skills that are important in decision making and data response papers. However you should not feel abashed if your intention is simply to make some lessons more challenging for the pupils and perhaps more interesting for you. This is really worth doing for its own sake.

The Style

We have had to make some difficult decisions in writing this book—**because it is very different**. Nine teachers have been involved in writing. All the strategy write-ups have been edited to achieve some conformity in coverage and style, but there has been a deliberate decision not to make them all the same. We hope that this will give the impression that there is room for individuality and your own professional skill in planning and delivery. Therefore some write-ups give greater attention to launching, some to managing, and others to debriefing, depending on the emphasis employed by the teacher. We have not tried to pretend that everything went smoothly with all the trials, partly in the hope that you will not be too dismayed if your first experiences are not a brilliant success. Over time, you will learn to make these strategies work effectively. However, we hope that there are enough descriptions of excitement, confusion, insight and real learning to convince you that this is **geography with a difference.** The write-ups of the trials are provided to give you some guidelines to avoid predictable pitfalls and to make you think seriously about the issues you will have to address with your classes. They cannot be exact templates to give you instant success. We hope that we are providing you with some materials and scaffolding, but you still have to build the house.

The use of the words 'student' and 'pupil' is not consistent throughout the book; the use in exemplars reflects the age group with which the teacher was working.

In some exemplars the teacher has stuck to describing what she/he did in the past tense. In others, the writer has adopted a future tense—'you should'. The latter is a sign that the teacher has used this strategy in a variety of contexts on numerous occasions and feels more certain about generalising advice. The former suggests less experience with the strategy, and therefore less certainty.

Rationale

The rationale, written as a general introduction to each strategy, gives a broad view of the value of the strategy and/or the personal motivation of the teacher for using it. It is not written to persuade you of the correctness of one particular view but rather to help you think about the potential relevance and power of the strategy as you watch the students engage with it and talk about it afterwards.

The following headings are used for each exemplar:

Context

This gives the background to the class and the topic with which the strategy was used. It gives some idea of the content/teaching that had gone before and some of the characteristics of the class. However, in most cases, matching the preceding content is not vital. What has gone before can alter both the way the activity proceeds, and the outcomes. For example, a ***Living Graph*** can be used at the end of a module to help pupils make connections between separate knowledge items and thus consolidate their understanding, but it could also be used at the beginning to stimulate a class and to raise questions which can form the core of an enquiry.

Precise behavioural objectives are not given because we feel that the activities do not fit a linear learning model and do not have simple behavioural outcomes that can be predetermined. It is very hard to say what pupils will learn; they are being provided with learning experiences and some of the purposes of the debriefing are to **find out what they have learned,** to help them identify it; to give it a name and to demonstrate its importance and relevance. Therefore we prefer to talk about **possible learning outcomes**. It does help preparation if you have some idea about what they might learn, but you always have to be on the lookout for the unexpected. However we do not imply that objectives cannot or should not be written for lessons using these materials, rather that their exact nature will depend upon the context.

Preparation

This section contains suggestions about what could/should be done before the lesson to make it run smoothly and to give you maximum chance of success. This does not excuse you from planning the lesson in some detail. These strategies and exemplars are not worksheets or simple textbooks that can be dished out and used with no thought. They are not teacher-proof. We would expect some teachers to rewrite some of the materials so that they will fit their particular context better. When you take up something new and different you need to go back to square one and not take too much for granted. More specifically you might need to:

- think about the *launching*;
- have a written note of what *instructions* you will give and perhaps refer to it during the lesson;
- think about the *managing* of the activity, so that you support and encourage but don't interfere too much;
- plan the *debriefing*, (so that you have some time for it at least), know some of the questions you will ask, and give some thought to how you will respond to anything pupils say;
- prepare some *follow-up* work.

Launching

The first time that you use a strategy with a class you may need to persuade them to accept the relevance and the different demands being made. This is especially the case if they are used to a diet of undemanding lessons with correct answers. These activities can make students feel threatened because they are unfamiliar. We have used the word **launching** to establish a particular analogy: a boat is stationary on a slipway; the chocks/brakes are removed; you give it a shove and it gathers momentum down the slipway. You are giving the students a shove, and they gather speed because **thinking** is something natural which we enjoy (unless we have learned to steer clear of it). It enters the water (a new medium) and with a bit of luck it floats freely and independently, ie, the students start to think for themselves as they do the task. The debriefing process can be likened to the boat being fitted out so that it is thoroughly seaworthy, with all its equipment and trained crew (thinking resources and strategies—students become independent learners!). As you will appreciate, this does not happen in one lesson and you have to launch the boat over and over again. You will notice in some write-ups that where classes had been exposed to either that strategy or others before, launching was less of an issue because the boat was already floating.

Instructions

This section outlines the instructions that will help you avoid a few of the pitfalls, but of course instructions are not all given to the pupils in one big slab. Some were committed to paper in the trials, in which case these sheets are included, but in other cases they were given verbally.

Managing the activity

Perhaps the single most useful piece of advice here is to think about your intentions for the particular activity. To some extent you will be concerned with the learning of content, because the activities are not content free: therefore you will have some regard to this. But overall your paramount concern should be with developing the students as learners. If you interfere too much or unnecessarily you will stunt their growth; if you leave them stranded they will not make any progress and they will get frustrated. This uneasy middle point has been termed **contingent teaching**, providing just enough support to encourage pupils to engage and learn but not too much so that they use you as a crutch and learn nothing (another term used in similar contexts is **scaffolding**). We all have to forgive ourselves for getting this wrong at times. Nonetheless, each strategy write-up contains useful, practical advice about making that strategy work well.

Debriefing

This is the very hardest part of teaching thinking to get right, but at the same time it is the most crucial. You need to determine whether the lesson was not only interesting and challenging (good in itself) but whether you have also gone further, and enabled the pupils to consolidate the learning and transfer it to other contexts. This is the **multiplier factor**.

Not all of the exemplars have details about debriefing: either the teacher felt that it was not appropriate or because circumstances, such as time, ruled it out. For our purposes here it is useful to talk about four possible strands to debriefing:

- get pupils to explain their answer/solution at length;
- ask pupils about their mental processes as they did a task or tackled a problem;
- ask pupils about the patterns in reasoning that they employed, or which emerged in discussion (these two constitute **thinking about thinking** or **metacognition**).
- draw the attention of pupils to other contexts where the same reasoning is valuable. These may be in other topics in geography, in other subjects or in their everyday lives. This is termed **bridging** and the intention is to get them to transfer their learning from the geography lesson to the other contexts.

All the contributors to this book find debriefing a difficult practice to establish for a variety of reasons. Some are logistical (ie, fitting it into a packed lesson) and some are intellectual (ie, hard for pupils to engage in). This book therefore limits its ambitions in relation to debriefing; we hope to be able to get you to do some, or to make a start at least.

Follow-up

Many, but not all, of the strategies have some suggestions for follow-up activities. Decisions on follow-up activities have to be taken in the context of the objectives of the lesson or unit in which the exemplars or strategies are used. There is an issue often about how to turn good thinking into writing. Good advice in this area can be found in Christine Counsell's Historical Association publication (1997) which is easily applied to geography.

Adapting the Strategy

After the three exemplars some general advice is given on how you might approach adapting the strategy to other geography teaching contexts, eg, suitable topics, finding source material, writing resources, variations on the tasks and instructions.

Afterthoughts

'Afterthoughts' gives some final reflections by the teacher(s) on what they have learned from using the strategy. Using these strategies with any degree of success is a form of professional development in itself. There are also some comments relating to getting other members of staff to use the strategy.

Teaching Thinking and the National Curriculum

The revised National Curriculum for Key Stage 3 published in 2000 introduced five embedded thinking skills to be taught in all subjects. Whilst there can always be debate about the detail of such lists, they clearly provide an important language for planning and teaching in the foreseeable future.

The Table of Exemplars on page iii can be used to help you plan when and how to use the materials in *Thinking Through Geography*.

Odd One Out

Rationale

Many games make an excellent framework for thinking strategies. After all, games are mostly enjoyable and they make you think a bit. It is worth reflecting on the number of important skills that are employed in playing Monopoly well, to say nothing of Bridge. *Odd One Out* draws on the heritage of good games, by getting students to think about the characteristics of things.

Unless one can identify the most important characteristics of a phenomenon then one cannot classify it and one will not describe it well or associate it with other important related information. The major concept being addressed therefore is **classification**.

> *Classification is a fundamental concept because the mastery of all other concepts rests upon it.*

The strategy uses a very simple format in asking students to pick the odd one out from a list of words, although as you will see there a number of variations on the basic theme. It can be used at the beginning of a topic as a starting point to see what students already know, or perhaps more effectively, as an end point to assess and revise a unit.

The advantages and strengths may be summarised as follows:

- students become more familiar with the meanings of key vocabulary, related to the characteristics that help pick the *Odd One Out* (eg, processes, landforms, erosion, deposition, features, causes and effects). This heightened awareness is very important during revision so that students understand examination questions;

> *Having a secure vocabulary in the subject is both demanded by KS3 PoS (para 3g) and vital to good examination performance —thinking is not content free.*

- students are encouraged to see the similarities and differences between key terms, rather than seeing them as a collection of disconnected words. As a result they get a bigger picture of the topic;

- it is good fun and makes the teacher think as much as the pupils;

- it can be done quickly, in as little as 10-15 minutes, and in a variety of student groupings, which makes it very flexible (ie, it could be used as an extension task for fast finishers, a paired task as one activity in a lesson, or as a whole lesson activity);

- as it is fairly easy to make *Odd One Out* work, it is really interesting to go round and listen to students—you get a window into how they think;

> *Being able to listen to students is vital to successful debriefing.*

- it is easy to explain to other members of staff.

Odd One Out Exemplar 1: River basins and flooding

Context

This activity was used with a mixed ability Y7 group at the end of a unit of work on river basins and flooding. They were generally a noisy and lively group, demanding of teacher time, and the class included some pupils with considerable learning difficulties. Within the topic the pupils had studied features of river basins, the water cycle, movement of water and causes and effects of flooding (paras 8a and 8b in PoS). The activity was planned to be a basic test of terminology and the pupils' ability to relate the terms to each other. Actually it turned out to be much more.

Preparation

Very little physical preparation is required, apart from duplicating the wordsheets. You need to give some thought to the tasks that you will use and to the word sets that you give to the pupils, so that you have decided which is your odd one out and why. (They may of course come up with a legitimate alternative.) You should work out your response to the tasks on the instruction sheet and, if you feel uneasy about the sets, change them.

We have developed five variants of the task beyond the standard form, and they can be considered when preparing the lesson:

1. **Brainstorming** the words at the start of the activity. Use the board and do a bit of judicious editing. This variant is probably best left till you are more expert.
2. **Quick fire** rounds. Ask the whole class to work quickly on one set.
3. **Adding on**. Once they have identified the *Odd One Out*, ask the pupils to add another word to the set which has something in common. So for example having been given waterfall, solution and meander, pupils will usually choose solution as the *Odd One Out* on the grounds that it is a process not a landform; now they have to add on another landform.
4. Pupils **create their own sets**.
5. **Classification** of the whole list.

Not all the tasks need to be used but they represent a progression in the use of the resource, helping the students to build their skills and understanding.

Launching

The activity was introduced by telling the pupils that they were going to be playing a game, using words from the topic that they had been studying. Of course (if you had used it) you could refer to the *Classification* activity (see page 114) and tell the pupils that they were going to be using their brilliant classifying skills. A high impact alternative which would require more effort would be to hold up an apple, a banana, some grapes, and a carrot and ask which is the *Odd One Out*. If you get the expected answer, carrot, you can make the point that all were edible, full of vitamins and minerals and colourful (shared characteristics), but the carrot is not a fruit, it is a vegetable. You can make all sorts of jokes about what a fool you would look if you put carrot in a fruit salad and so on. By seeing the links between things that make them a group, we show wisdom and understanding and we keep our jobs as chefs!

In this case the pupils were given 2-3 minutes to brainstorm as many words as they could associate with the topic they had just finished, resulting in a spider diagram on the board. (They weren't allowed to use their books!!) Having done this, we completed 3 or 4 examples in the form of a quick fire round to get them warmed up, eg, 1, 23, 26—which is the Odd One Out? They got the idea very quickly.

Throughout the book, you are encouraged to use your professional judgement but this should not result in taking the challenge out of activities (see page 159).

This is a simple introduction to metacognition (see page 159)...thinking about learning.

This may be seen as an example of bridging into the activity, which helps pupils see a more general value to the activity.

Instructions

1. Distribute the pre-prepared word list—(which of course varied slightly from the one on the board). Give the Instructions sheet to pairs. Ask the pupils to read through them quickly.

2. Read through Task 1. Explain that the numbers are used as a reference system for the words on the wordsheet and that everyone must be able to see both the instructions and the wordsheet.

3. Explain that each list of words (as indicated by the numbers) has an 'Odd One Out', and that they have to decide what it is. Stress the importance of being able to say **why** and that you are looking for straightforward 'geography-type' answers and not wacky ones (this may happen with some able pupils). Tell them to write down their answer including the reason.

4. Emphasise the importance of discussing and agreeing in the pair before writing anything down: either partner must be able to explain their answer.

> **Odd One Out Exemplar 1: River basins and flooding**

Managing the activity

From experience of using this strategy a number of times it has been found that pairs are the most suitable grouping. Pairs are supportive and this activity does not need the resources of a larger group. The first time pupils do this they tend to lack confidence about what is expected and they need considerable reassurance that they are doing the tasks correctly.

This is just one example of many of the roles of talk in aiding understanding (see page 160).

Timing of the activity is fairly flexible. Left to their own devices, pairs will work at very different rates, not because they are being idle but rather because some talk things through in greater detail and look for alternatives. You may prefer to let them work at their own speed or to tell them to move on to the next task every few minutes. It is a missed opportunity if you do not move the class on to Task 4 at some point as this is a higher order task which capitalises on the understanding generated in the earlier tasks.

Some pupils only did Task 3 or Task 4 and some did the whole lot, which did not detract from the overall value of the activity. We were not only looking for correct answers, but also for fundamental understanding. Some had the attitude that this was just a game, with little to do with geography, but as we discussed this they began to change their minds.

Debriefing

Debriefing was limited in this case. We went over their answers and cleared up some misconceptions (which was valuable in itself). Over the course of this phase we kept coming back to very important words (such as process and landform, hazards, flood defences, upland and lowland) which was a central purpose of the lesson.

This is one example of differentiation by outcome.

Follow-up

This is outlined on the instruction sheet.

Odd One Out Exemplar 1: River basins and flooding

Wordsheet—River basins and flooding

1. Evaporation	18. Drought
2. Tarmac	19. Stores
3. Grass	20. Tidal waves
4. Planting trees	21. Slope
5. Watershed	22. Lake
6. Heavy rain	23. Precipitation
7. Transfers	24. Sand
8. High tides	25. Deforestation
9. Monsoons	26. Typhoons
10. Vegetation	27. Mouth
11. Drainage basin	28. Channel
12. Condensation	29. Groundwater
13. Concrete	30. Surface water
14. Urbanisation	31. Snowmelt
15. Dam building	32. Raising river banks
16. Source	33. Throughflow
17. Tributary	

Instructions

Odd One Out Exemplar 1: River basins and flooding

You have been given a list of words which you might have come across during your work on *Rivers and Flooding*. You are going to use these words to complete the following tasks.

Task 1

Working with a partner, look at the sets of numbers below, which match to a word from the list on the wordsheet. Pick out the words and write them in your book. Then try to decide which word from each set is the *Odd One Out*. Underline this word in your book and explain why it is the *Odd One Out* and what the other two have in common.

Set A	2	13	3
Set B	4	15	6
Set C	8	27	31
Set D	22	10	25
Set E	1	12	14
Set F	30	11	29
Set G	14	20	32
Set H	31	20	8
Set I	23	28	17
Set J	5	16	19

Task 2

Now that you have started to see a pattern, add an extra word to each group, but keep the same *Odd One Out*.

Task 3

Now try to put together your own group of words with an *Odd One Out*, and you must have a good and obvious reason. Swap your group of words with your partner and see if they can work yours out and vice versa.

Task 4

Now try to sort out all the words from the list on the wordsheet into 4 to 6 groups.

Odd One Out Exemplar 2: Traffic management

Cause and effect are two of the big concepts elaborated in Appendix 1 (see page 167).

It should be remembered that, despite the instructions, these activities still need careful planning.

Context

This was used with a Y10 GCSE class who had never done an *Odd One Out* before. They were following the NEAB syllabus 'C' and had got to the section on traffic and movement. Most recently, pupils had been studying traffic problems and commuting in Blyth and Tyneside, and this was used as a summary activity. The intention was both to revise the unit and to develop pupils' awareness of such terms as cause, effect and traffic management.

Preparation

Nothing physical is required beyond the most obvious step of duplicating the sheets. However, as with any *Odd One Out*, it really repays if you sit down and think through the important categories so that you can respond to the pupils more intelligently. We have been deliberate in not giving you our reasoning behind the selection of numbers; we want you to think them through and if necessary work out your own sets. However we should make it clear that some sets are designed around causal links rather than shared characteristics. The set of **10** (rush hour), **12** (pedestrian crossing), **26** (double yellow lines) and **29** (accident) is deliberately ambiguous. It can be argued that the rush hour leads to accidents, which has led to pedestrian crossings being installed. But another explanation is that pedestrian crossings and double yellow lines are intended to reduce accidents, which leaves rush hour as *Odd One Out*.

Launching

If you have a class which has not done an *Odd One Out* before, go through one set of words with them or use some of the activities for launching in Exemplar 1.

Instructions

They worked in pairs using the instructions on the sheet.

Managing the activity

This was easy. The pupils were totally absorbed and I had the chance to listen and answer questions. Not everyone knew what pedestrianisation was; photochemical smog needed some explanation; most did not associate dust particles with exhaust fumes and some took sleeping policemen literally! Some of these explanations might have been avoided if I had asked them to read through the words for 2 minutes at the beginning and asked for questions of clarification, but failing to do this did not detract from the lesson, which was a pleasure. The pupils were thoughtful and inventive, especially in Tasks 3 and 4. Only a few made deliberately daft suggestions.

In this instance, the level of challenge was appropriate.

Debriefing

In the debriefing I focused on Task 4, where the pupils were asked to devise 3-6 categories. They had been forced to think really hard and it proved to be a very effective way of making them consider traffic management. Some pupils had seriously looked at different ways that they could form groups.

There were several common headings:
- materials (concrete);
- movement (tidal flows, school runs);
- problems;
- solutions;
- effects;

- cars;
- parking;
- rush hour;
- causes.

The pupils could make little of the question about how they had formed the groups. They agreed that problems, causes and solutions were the most useful headings and that solutions could be usefully split into concrete and non-concrete. They thought the activity was useful on two grounds:

- firstly they had been forced to think about the meaning of all the words and not just accept them;
- secondly they had to work out the categories, they would remember them much better than if they had just copied from a book.

I made the point that many other issues and topics could be looked at in this way—problems, causes, effects, solutions—for instance, residential environments, which they had already studied.

> **Odd One Out Exemplar 2: Traffic management**

> *The pupils have constructed their own understanding rather than just being told (see page 157).*

> *A limited example of bridging (see page 162).*

Odd One Out Exemplar 2: Traffic management

Wordsheet—Traffic management

1. Cycle track	18. Speed cameras
2. Wheel clamp	19. Bus passes
3. Exhaust fumes	20. Bypass
4. Park and ride	21. Intersection/junction
5. Inner-urban motorway	22. Bus lanes
6. Vibration damage	23. Road rage
7. One-way street	24. Sleeping policemen
8. Journey to work	25. Multi-storey car parks
9. Tailbacks	26. Double yellow lines
10. Rush hour	27. Pedestrianised streets
11. Rapid transit system	28. Photochemical smog
12. Pedestrian crossing	29. Accidents
13. Tidal flow	30. Dust particles
14. Noise	31. School runs
15. Roundabouts	32. Taxis
16. Petrol consumption	33. Ring road
17. Shopping trips	34. Congestion

Instructions

Odd One Out Exemplar 2: Traffic management

Task 1

Each of the numbers in the sets of four below relates to a word to do with traffic in urban areas. Can you work out with your partner which one is the *Odd One Out* and what connects the other three?

Set A	8	15	17	31
Set B	4	17	19	33
Set C	5	11	22	32
Set D	10	12	26	29
Set E	2	9	18	24
Set F	14	28	30	31
Set G	1	13	16	34

Task 2

Still with your partner, can you find *one more* from the wordsheet to add to *each* of the sets above so that all *four* items have something in common, but the *Odd One Out* remains the same? Think about why you have chosen each one.

Task 3

Now it's your turn to design some sets to try out on your partner! Choose three numbers that you think have something in common with each other and one that you think has nothing to do with the other three. Get your partner to find the *Odd One Out*, then do one of theirs. Try a few each, but remember to be reasonable.

Task 4

Can you organise all the words into groups. You are allowed to create between 3 and 6 groups and each group must be given a descriptive heading that unites the words in the group. Try not to have any left over. Be prepared to rethink as you go along.

Odd One Out Exemplar 3: Population and migration

Context

The lucky class who got to do this was a Y9 group, after 3 weeks studying demographic transition, population problems and policies in a variety of countries at different levels of economic development. Although mixed ability, the class contained a large number of low achieving pupils—few had reading ages beyond their chronological age. I was particularly concerned that they should make links between the concepts that we had been looking at. The module had a central driving question: how have family sizes changed through recent generations of our own families, and why have these changes happened?

Preparation

As in other examples of *Odd One Out*.

Launching

This was different. I reactivated the main enquiry question. Pupils had done some homework on the size of families and living conditions in previous generations. From previous years I knew what to expect so I asked some questions to tap into accounts about siblings of (great) grandparents who had died, living conditions and leaving school (eg, at 13 or 14 to go down the pit). This provided an important context so that the class would start to think about the reasons for variations in birth rate.

Homework can be excellent preparation because, if pupils are working from knowledge they have gathered, they are more likely to develop understanding.

Having given out the wordsheets, I asked individual students to explain the connection between some pairs of terms (such as nutrition and infant mortality), taking care to pose easier pairs for the less able. Frequently they needed nudging towards full explanations, but it was important to demonstrate to the class the quality of responses expected, as a check on understanding and to correct some misapprehensions. For example, ageing and death rate were thought to be positively correlated by the pupil questioned until another argued the opposite. It seemed possible/likely that there would be a danger of mutual reinforcement of such misunderstandings, so I engineered pairings that put weaker pupils with a stronger partner. This would be particularly important when they designed their own sets.

Scaffolding, see page 160.

Instructions

These were contained in the sheet given to the pupils (ODD ONE OUT RESOURCE SHEET 5).

Managing the activity

Some pupils were unsettled by the thought that there was not a correct answer, so they needed some reassurance. As this *Odd One Out* is as much about causal connections as it is about characteristics, it took the group much longer to get going. Each one took longer and some groups needed a jump-start on some sets—it felt almost like wiring up their brains. They could not make a connection by themselves but once I had put the bits together for them there would be a little crackle, a few sparks, and they would splutter into life! One of these episodes would go something like this (using Set C **2 10 15 26**):

This is a superb example of a teacher attempting to move pupils through their Zone of Proximal Development, ZPD (see page 159).

Me:	*Stuck?*
Group:	*Yes.*
Me:	*OK... Age of marriage and birth rates.* [They look blank]. *If people get married young, say 18, they have got perhaps 25 years in which to have children...OK?* [They nod]. *If people get married at*

>   30, they have only got 15 years to have children...
>   OK? [They nod]. So if they get married younger, are
>   they likely to have more or less children?
>
> **Group:**   More?
>
> **Me:**   So, more children... is that a higher or lower birth
>   rate?
>
> **Group:**   [Sparks and flashes] Higher!
>
> **Me:**   Now careers...
>
> **Group member:** Yeah, if girls have a career they don't get married so
>   young... I get it. [Now they are going, they talk it
>   through.]

Odd One Out Exemplar 3: Population and migration

(It would have been valid for their particular community if they had made the point that you don't have to be married to have children.)

Some pairs did not need this, and I left them to it. The quality of discussion was excellent, and although there were some misapprehensions at large I heard some of these being sorted out in the groups. There was some comparing between groups; and because different connections had been made some pairs contested theirs against another. They were very clearly learning from each other.

In Task 3, when pupils had designed their own sets, they were allowed to be more specific (eg, *low* birthrate or *many* people per doctor) if their partner was struggling with a set. Several (more able) students felt constrained by the list of terms and were allowed to add new terms such as famine and divorce since they clearly understood some of the links to the rest. Both these examples are instances of effective differentiation. In fact, if you use its inherent flexibility, this activity is a brilliant approach to differentiation.

This is a potentially rich language environment likely to promote learning (see page 160).

Debriefing

This was similar to Exemplar 2 (see page 14).

Follow-up

This is contained within the list of Tasks (see ODD ONE OUT RESOURCE SHEET 6).

Odd One Out
Exemplar 3:
Population and migration

Wordsheet—Population and migration

1. Overcrowding	17. Drinking water
2. Age of marriage	18. Farm work
3. Rural areas	19. Ageing
4. Death rate	20. Push factors
5. Education	21. Natural increase
6. Infant mortality	22. Primary health care
7. Male inheritance	23. Industry
8. Pull factor	24. Sterilisation
9. Disease	25. Religion
10. Birth rate	26. Careers
11. Urban areas	27. People per doctor
12. Life expectancy	28. Less developed countries
13. Nutrition	29. More developed countries
14. Youthful	30. Obesity
15. Cholera	31. Contraception
16. Migration	32. Heart disease

Odd One Out
Exemplar 3:
Population and migration

Instructions

Task 1

Look at the sets of 4 words below and decide with your partner which is the *Odd One Out*. Make sure that you are clear about the reason and what connects the other three.

Set A	3	18	19	28
Set B	8	11	13	23
Set C	2	10	15	26
Set D	6	13	17	25
Set E	1	4	15	2

Task 2

Again with a partner, can you find one more from the list to add to each of the sets so that now four items have something in common, but the *Odd One Out* remains the same. Note down your reasons.

Task 3

Now it's your turn to design some sets to try out on your partner! Try to make them different from the ones that we have done already. When you are both ready, swap. Try a few each.

Task 4

Can you organise all the words into groups? You are allowed to create between 3 and 6 groups and each group must be given a descriptive heading or title. Try not to have any left over, so be prepared to change your mind.

Odd One Out: Adapting the strategy

This is perhaps the easiest strategy in the book to adapt to other contexts. The only hard part is generating the list of words. This is not quite as straightforward as it seems, because there has to be some thought behind your choice, in as much as you have to decide on the major categories of words or concepts that you wish to be 'discovered' by the students. If for example you were doing a list for coasts, it is advisable to decide which of the following categories to include, erosion processes, erosional landforms, depositional landforms, factors affecting coastal morphology, coastal management features, recreational uses of coastal areas, landforms associated with sea level changes, coastal management interest groups, etc.

The list of five variants of the game listed in preparation for the first exemplar also contains useful advice (page 10).

The words on the wordsheet should be numbered (for ease of reference) and typed out in a random order so that the students cannot see any pattern in the list. You need to prepare your word sets so that you have a view on which is the odd one out, although you have to be prepared to accept alternative answers as long as they are justified.

Afterthoughts

In planning, implementing and writing up this activity we have been forced to think about what we are asking the pupils to do and how important it is. We knew that it 'worked' well but we now begin to see some of its importance. For example, we can presently identify four kinds of relationships in the sets:

- sets that share an important characteristic, such as noise, exhaust fumes and dust particles (all pollutants from traffic);
- sets that are part of a causal chain such as rush hour, tail backs and road rage;
- sets which have a centre word which has separate links to two others, such as dam building, linked to concrete and stores;
- sets which form a web, of which there are many examples in the Population Exemplar, such as education, birth rate and careers. Here every member can be linked separately to the other two.

It is tempting to speculate on the importance of this type of activity. An immediate outcome is a better grasp of vocabulary, especially where the sets are based on shared characteristics. However, where the sets are based on causal links or webs, are the pupils being supported in developing their understanding of relationships? We are struck by the coincidence of what seemed to be happening as students worked on the task (and talked) and the geography level descriptions. Level 4 for instance includes:

> *'They recognise and describe physical and human processes. They begin to show understanding of how these processes can change the features of places, and that these changes affect the lives and activities of people living there.'*

> Level 7 progresses to *'They describe the interactions within and between physical and human processes. They show how these interactions create geographical patterns and contribute to change in places and patterns.'*

This might suggest that **Odd One Out** would make an excellent assessment tool—an issue worth researching in the future.

Living Graphs

Rationale

This is one of the simpler activities to plan and manage, but its outcomes are profound. Students draw or are given a preprinted line graph. They are given a number of statements relating to events or things people might have said that relate to the context of the graph and they have to decide where on the graph (at what time point) it was most likely to have occurred.

Geography uses graphs as one of its stock-in-trade techniques, and when students are presented with them in lessons they are usually asked simple data response questions or to describe the graph, or maybe they are just asked to draw a graph from a set of data. These tasks have their place. They develop a familiarity with and basic understanding of the properties of line graphs and give students crucial practice in the simple type of examination question. However, use of graphs rarely excites or creates debate and argument. Graphs can be relied on generally for bread and butter, undemanding lessons, in which we get a respite and students can get some satisfaction from a neat page.

Living Graphs change all that. They give the figures and the lines real context and allow students to make connections between the abstraction of the graph on the page and the people and events that lie behind it. While line graphs show the relationship between just two variables, such as time and population, *Living Graphs* give a reminder that other variables, such as migration and public health are interacting with the ones depicted in the graph. Therefore they greatly assist students in constructing meaning from the graph.

> *This process may result in cognitive conflict for some students (see page 159).*

Living Graphs make students think and talk and disagree with each other and you. They encourage them to ask more questions and even on occasions to stay behind after the bell. They make students look at graphs in a totally new light. They are extremely flexible and exactly the same resources can be used for a Y7 and a Y13 class, which says much about their potential for differentiation by outcome.

Living Graphs Exemplar 1: The demographic transition model

Here is another example that Thinking Skills activities do not jeopardise geographic content—they just use it better.

Context

This was used with a very mixed ability Y10 group in a unit on population. It had the complete spectrum of students: attention seekers, quiet but hard working students, lazy students, half a dozen very able students of varying dispositions and statemented students including a deaf pupil with ancillary support. They had covered birth, death and fertility rates and how these related to population change, and they had studied migration. They were a slightly unpredictable group who can respond well or prove difficult (for no obvious reason).

I was concerned that they should come to the living graph exercise already having a good grasp of how and why Britain's population had changed since 1820. Therefore I planned a long lead in (which took longer than expected) in which they had to plot birth rates (BR) and death rates (DR) for Britain from 1821 to 1981. Using descriptive data they then had to plot the population. Basically if BR and DR were close, population growth would be fairly gentle, but if BR greatly exceeded DR the steepness of the line would be much greater.

The living graph statements were printed on the RESOURCE SHEETS that students were working from, but are reproduced separately here. It should be noted that the statements relate particularly to a British context.

Preparation

You will need to prepare, or get the students to draw, a copy of the Demographic Transition Model graph or a graph of birth rates, death rates and population for Britain since c1800. Such graphs can be found in many textbooks. I felt that it would be very important to be able to point to the graph as they explained where they had put the statements so I prepared an OHP.

Launching

There was nothing special required to get the task done. It was just one task on a sheet amongst others and as students got to that point I just checked that they knew what to do. In fact, most got to the task near the end of the first of the two lessons that this activity spanned. Launching seems much less necessary for this activity than for many others because graphs are so familiar. In none of the three exemplars was launching a high priority. With some classes and contexts you might need to pay more attention to this, but for us it has never been a necessity.

Instructions

At the beginning of the second lesson I went over the task again. My main concern was to convey that a variety of positions on the graph was possible, so I went through one statement with them and gave two different justifications for placing that statement in two completely different places.

This action both helps to scaffold and maintains the essential ambiguity.

Managing the activity

There were two subtle aspects to this.

- There was a temptation among a few just to copy what a neighbour had done, because they thought it was too difficult or it must have a catch, so I had to stress that there were no right answers. I encouraged them to ask if they were not sure what a statement implied or meant, but otherwise they must think for themselves.

- On the other hand, a few gave it virtually no thought and just put down the first thing that came into their heads, not allowing for the possibility that this was ambiguous and that there was a variety of possible interpretations. Therefore I tried to press a few students to think a bit more about their answers.

Debriefing

This was the first time that the class had done a living graph. When we got to the whole class discussion (debriefing) they began to realise that the task had much more depth and was more complex than they first appreciated—they had seen it as just another task on a worksheet. From my experiences with other classes, the return from using the strategy is cumulative, ie, they get more from doing them when they have done a few.

Actually, nearly all the tough management issues were loaded into the debriefing, which threw up several surprises.

The debriefing was allocated 20 minutes which, in the end, was not enough, because the students extended the discussion and used up much more time than I had expected. In fact we only discussed about half the statements. Is it practical to give up much more time? You could argue that learning needs to be talked about at length and it has been claimed that time should be evenly split between debriefing and teaching activities. For many groups this would not be practical. Perhaps the answer is that 20 minute spells of debriefing get built-in over the whole course and therefore it does not matter whether every last drop is squeezed out of an activity.

Returning to this activity we went through a number of statements in detail. I asked particular students to say where they had put the statement and why. Sometimes they were really stumped and there were awkward silences. Sometimes I got some very sensible but fairly short responses and sometimes I got very lengthy, provocative responses that I had to think carefully about and seek clarification on from the pupil. Sometimes the discussion went right out of my hands as a couple of students discussed a point between them. It was noticeable that the main volunteers were the brightest girl and two boys who usually spend most of their time causing trouble. I suspect that some of the boys' contributions were designed to wind me up, but actually they were generally making thoughtful contributions, either speculating in interesting ways or making tangential connections to other topics. For example, one boy asked when houses in Britain started to have heating, because children sleeping in one bed could be a response to the cold rather than high birth rates. In another instance, a girl mentioned that thinking about family planning must be related to education in a variety of ways, and a boy chipped in that farmers probably had many children to provide a cheap workforce. I have some doubts about what was going on in the minds of the students who said nothing, but this applies equally to class discussions in general.

Follow-up

Remember that in the sequence described so far the students had not been introduced to the term *Demographic Transition Model* (DTM). Therefore the follow-up was designed to embed an understanding of the model in the work on population change (and associated changes in BRs and DRs).

The students were shown an OHP with the DTM on it. They were asked as a whole class what were the differences between it and the graph of British population (LIVING GRAPHS RESOURCE SHEET 2). This led to an explanation that it could be used to describe or predict the probable changes in the population growth in a country over time as it went through the process of economic development. It could also be used as a framework to compare countries at a particular date, showing that they were at different stages.

The point was made that there are factors operating in every country that meant that they would not exactly fit the model. Reference was made to the migration from Britain to the colonies in the 1800s which reduced the population increase. Similarly good medical care introduced into developing economies can speed up progress through the stages. The living graph activity was crucial here, because it had made them think about how various factors related to population change.

The students were then provided with statements based on an Action Aid pack *How Many Children?* (an excellent resource), taken from interviews with people in developing economies. Although focused on the issue of birth rate it provided some insight into the nature of the factors affecting population growth in those countries. They were asked to decide at what stage of the DTM these statements might occur—a second living graph exercise.

Living Graphs Exemplar 1: The demographic transition model

Teachers are faced with tough logistical problems in Thinking Skills, but if you always take the easy option, the potential benefits are reduced (see graph on page 166.)

This must be taken as a sign of success.

Speculating is a good quality talk marker (see page 160).

26

Living Graphs Exemplar 1: The demographic transition model

Statements—The demographic transition model

Task

Place these statements in the most appropriate place on the graph:

1.	Billy White loses his job as a gravedigger.
2.	Parents start to think more about family planning.
3.	Children are warmer in bed at night because they have more brothers and sisters.
4.	There are more Golden Weddings.
5.	A mother sobs over the grave of the last of her six children who died in a typhoid epidemic.
6.	A lot more houses are being built.
7.	The public health inspector smiles as the building of the new sewers is finished.
8.	Fewer children share a bedroom.
9.	Grandparents are rare.
10.	People are encouraged to emigrate to the colonies.

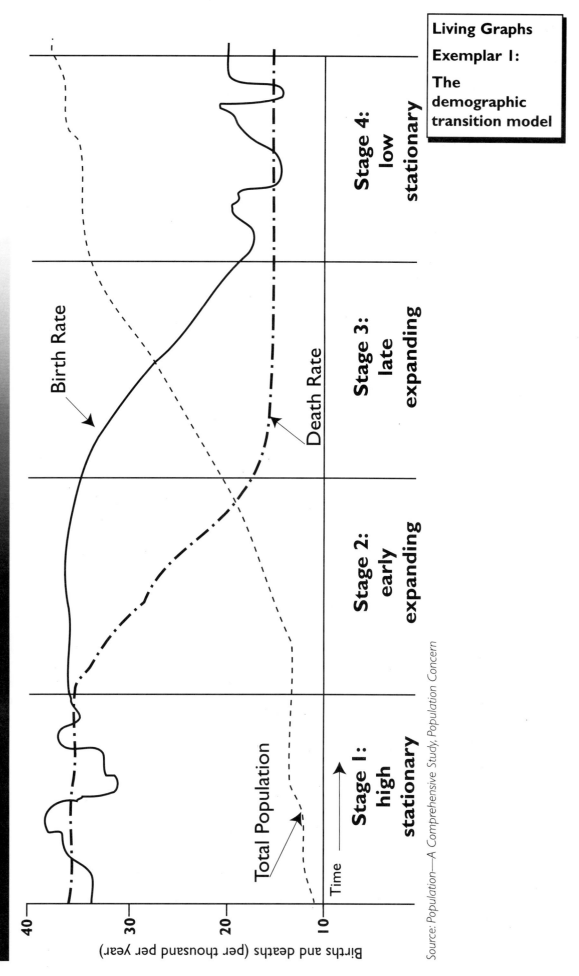

Living Graphs Exemplar 2: Daily energy consumption

Context

This activity was done with a Y7 mixed ability class, who were 'nice' and prepared to try new things. As it was their first experience of a *Living Graph* it was appropriate that it was a simple task with few statements to place. The unit of work was on energy, derived from para 15e of the NC Orders. This module was based on a number of questions, such as *'Why do people need energy? When do they use it? What forms does it take? Where does it come from?'* This activity came early in the teaching sequence and related particularly to the first two questions.

Preparation

The task was devised by a PGCE student (Chris Reid) from Newcastle University and was used by most of the departmental staff. I had to do four things.

1. Trace an outline graph from the original and duplicate it so that each pupil had one on which to locate the statements (LIVING GRAPHS RESOURCE SHEETS 3 and 4).
2. Duplicate a sheet with the statements (LIVING GRAPHS RESOURCE SHEET 5);
3. Prepare a sheet with only the axes so that pupils could do the homework on weekend electricity demand—see Follow-up (LIVING GRAPHS RESOURCE SHEET 6).
4. Prepare an OHP of the original graph (LIVING GRAPHS RESOURCE SHEET 3).

As it was the first time that this class had done a *Living Graph* I gave some thought to the clear instructions that they would need.

Launching

Although it was not crucial to the success of the activity, I started the lesson somewhat differently from usual. When the class arrived, I had the lights off and the blackout curtains drawn. As they came in one pupil put the light on. Once they were seated I asked him why he had done it. He replied that it was dark. I made the point to the class that Richard had had a reason for putting the light on and during the lesson we would be looking at the reasons why people use electricity when they do. This took no more than a minute.

Instructions

1. I gave out the original graph, the simplified version, and the statements (LIVING GRAPHS RESOURCE SHEETS 3, 4 and 5). I thought about keeping back the statements, but decided against this.
2. I explained what the graph showed. I reminded them that the horizontal axis was time using the 24 hour clock. I asked a couple of questions around this, eg, *'What time is 14.30 and 20.30?'* I was not convinced that every pupil could handle this, but I relied upon the more able to support the weaker ones. I told them not to worry about what GW meant on the vertical axis, it was just the amount of electricity being used.
3. I then asked a series of questions to improve their comprehension of the graph, eg, *'What is domestic? What is Economy 7? Why was the amount used greater in December than in November? What do the lines show?'* This was valuable because it emerged that some thought electricity demand would be greater at night because the lights were on.
4. Turning to the statements and the blank graph I explained that they had to decide where on the graph each statement should be put. I stressed that for some there was a right answer because there was a time stated, but for others there could be several different possibilities. The

Differentiation by group work.

The whole of this phase of the lesson helps to invoke their knowledge ready to be used in activity (see page 157).

important thing was to have a reason. They also needed to think about why the activity in the statement used electricity.

5. We did the first one together. As none of them raised the point, I asked why it was Mrs Jones and not Mr Jones. We had a little chat about whose dad did any cooking—fortunately there were some good role models. Then I told them to get on. I allowed them to work in the natural groups around the tables that they were working at—the group size varied from 2 to 4 pupils.

Living Graphs Exemplar 2: Daily energy consumption

Managing the activity

Much of the detail from the first exemplar applies here too, but they were very enthusiastic and I did not have a problem in keeping them on task. They asked a lot of questions as I went round. I tried not to influence them but when I saw a statement put in an inappropriate place I said something like *'Explain that one to me'*.

Pupils asking questions is a very healthy sign— when they are beyond 'How do I do this?'

Those who finished ahead of the rest were asked to make up 3 or 4 statements of their own, which they really enjoyed doing.

Debriefing

This took the form of asking what they had put and why. Statement number 4 caused the most difficulty, but it led to a good discussion about the electricity companies trying to persuade people to use electricity at night in storage heaters, etc (which a few had). One boy asked what happened to electricity that was not used, which totally stumped me. The activity showed that they had a good understanding of what the graph showed and they really liked the statement about the teacher marking books.

I wound this part up by asking what problem might arise during very cold weather in the middle of winter.

Follow-up

The follow-up was homework, which I spent at least 5 minutes explaining. Pupils were given the outline graph (Demand for electricity on a winter Sunday) with just the axes on (LIVING GRAPHS RESOURCE SHEET, 6). They had to draw in the line for electricity use on a winter Sunday and make up 4 statements to go on their graph. I talked through with them what was different about Sundays compared to a weekday. They loved the idea of making up their own line and statements. I think that it was the most popular homework of the year. This resulted in some excellent work (getting up late, Sunday roasts, etc) although a few of the weaker pupils were 'off-beam'.

This is an example of near transfer (see page 162).

Living Graphs Exemplar 2: Daily energy consumption

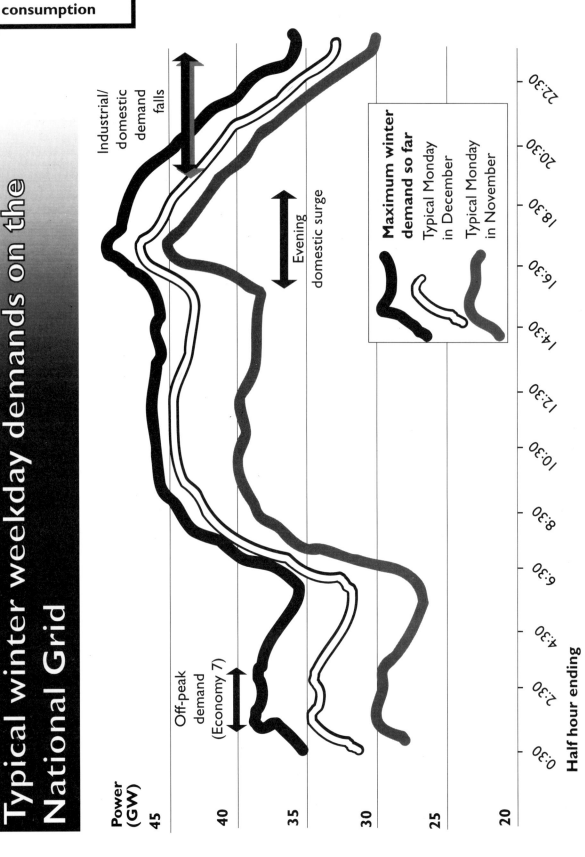

Typical winter weekday demands on the National Grid

Source: NGC demand forecasting

Living Graphs Exemplar 2: Daily energy consumption

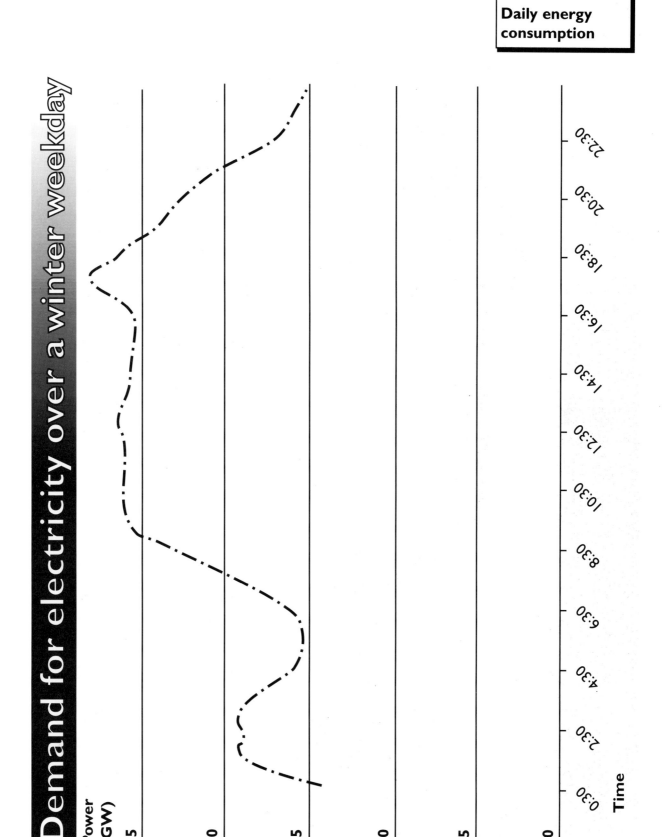

Living Graphs Exemplar 2: Daily energy consumption

Statements—Demand for electricity over a day

Task

Put the following statements on the graph:

1.	Mrs Sheila Jones arrives home from work and starts to cook the evening meal.
2.	Miss Terri Frain gets up after a hard night marking history books and has her first cup of coffee.
3.	Mr Allan Smith, an office clerk, takes the Metro (a train) from Newcastle city centre to South Shields during his lunchtime to deliver some important documents.
4.	The Robinson's washing machine switches on automatically on the timer.
5.	Patsy McBride, age 11, switches off the TV and bedside light in her room.
6.	Jane Thompson arrives at work at an insurance office.
7.	In the power station control room they reduce the output.

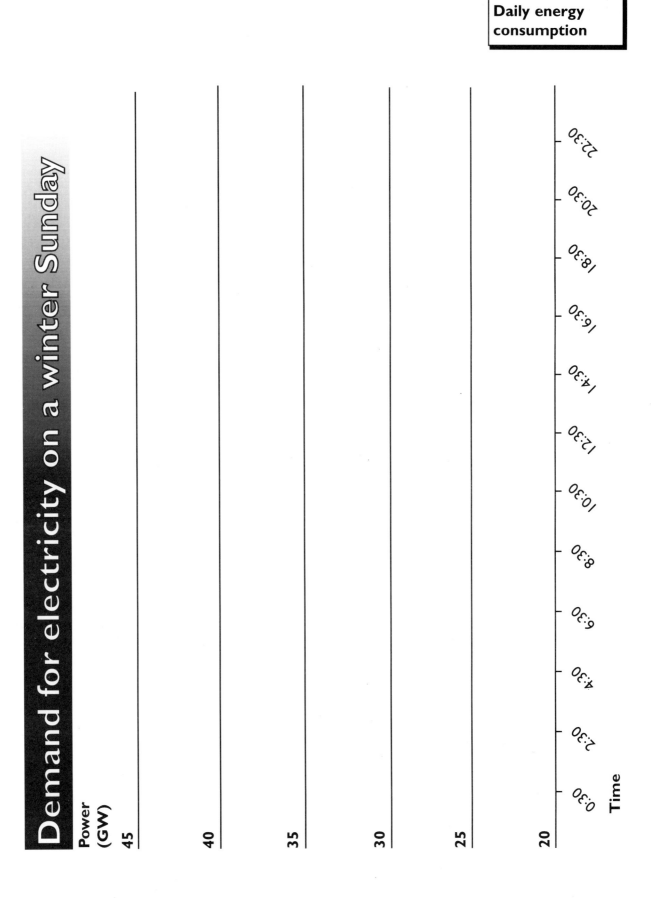

Living Graphs Exemplar 3: The stage model of tourism

Context

The trial group for this activity was a middle band Y8, with an inclination to be noisy and difficult to keep on task because of a short attention span. The work occurred in a unit on tourism which touched on several paragraphs of the NC Orders. The unit had started with an analysis of the factors which influence holiday destinations, drawing on their own holidays or desired holidays. They had watched a *Geographical Eye* programme on Torremolinos, and I had focused their attention onto why people want to go there and what they do when they get there. I had made the point that tourism is a major industry in Spain: it is vital to the economy and the government does much to encourage and protect the industry.

Preparation

The only preparation required is to duplicate the resource sheets with the statements and the blank graph (LIVING GRAPHS RESOURCE SHEETS 7 and 8). A textbook that covers tourism and has photographs can be a useful addition, especially if you have not done preliminary work as described in the context section. You could replace the stage model with a graph of the number of beds or hotels or tourist visitors to a resort.

Launching

No special effort was made but (if you are inclined) personal stories or photographs that contrast unspoilt holiday locations with those that are frayed round the edges could be a good starting point.

We looked at the Stage Model of Tourism in Waugh's *The World* and talked through what the stages implied.

Instructions

This group had done a living graph before, so instructions did not need to be elaborate. I reminded them of the one that they had done before. I also reminded them that there could be a variety of acceptable answers, so the important thing was to have good reasons for the position of any of the statements. Because the horizontal axis has only four stages, I encouraged them to consider whether the statement should be at the start, in the middle or at the end of a stage. I encouraged them to work as groups, but I did not organise this myself.

Managing the activity

Differentiation by outcome.

Some groups worked faster then others (which need not cause a problem) and was not directly related to ability but more to the depth of thought and discussion applied. I was impressed by the level of thinking of some of the less successful writers, for instance. They clearly enjoyed the task and I did not have to worry at all about pupils being off task. Some groups asked what certain words (such as ornithologist) meant and I made sure that I broadcast my answer so that everyone could hear. I gave the class 5 minutes after the first group had finished, and in the meantime I asked the fastest group to compose and locate 4 statements of their own.

Differentiation by extension task.

Follow-up

Less able groups might be helped by using writing frames (see page 81).

As a follow-up task they had to pick 4 statements, one from each stage, and explain why they had put it in that stage. They were encouraged to write at length and I stressed that it was to show whether they understood the graph. The work was very good. The answers were longer than I would normally expect, which reflected the thought that had been generated by the activity.

Debriefing

I asked what they had had to do to locate the statements on the graph. There was a general *'think about it'* response, but I pressed further by asking *'How?'* One girl said that she imagined it, which she explained involved having pictures in her mind stimulated by the statement. This started the class off and they chipped in with what their pictures had been and where they had come from—the video we had watched, their holidays, tour operator brochures, stories from books and the film *Shirley Valentine*. I made the point that we have to work at interpreting graphs, and that relating a graph to our own knowledge and experience is important and valuable.

In using a similar graph with a GCSE class, I asked them to identify which statements had more to do with *causes* of the change in the character of resorts and which had more to do with the *effects*. They also identified positive and negative effects. Point out that one statement can represent both cause and effect of change (cumulative causation)—as in Carlos's litter picking job.

> **Living Graphs Exemplar 3: The stage model of tourism**

> *This is metacognition (see page 159).*

> *Cause and effect are vital big concepts in geography (see page 167).*

Living Graphs Exemplar 3: The stage model of tourism

Statements—Changes in tourism
Task

Put the following statements on the graph:

1.	Carlos, a fisherman, gets up early in order to take his boat out.
2.	Neil gets drunk one night and on the way back is mugged, losing all his money, credit card and his passport.
3.	Durta, a German tourist will not let her son go to get an ice cream because of the extremely busy roads.
4.	Miguel goes out to look for work. Only two years ago he had regular employment for the summer period that allowed him the luxury of not working for the rest of the year.
5.	Mercedes relaxes on an empty beach, after doing her chores, enjoying the afternoon summer sun.
6.	José is an ornithologist who now has to travel miles down the coast to see the birds that used to nest here.
7.	Linda and Andy decide not to go back to Torremolinos next year. Linda thought it was 'naff'.
8.	Juan gets a well paid job in the construction industry. Many of his friends also get jobs.
9.	Angela has difficulty finding somewhere to get her travellers' cheques changed into pesetas.
10.	Carlos gets a job picking up litter off the beach every evening.
11.	The local farmers get better prices for their vegetables.
12.	The local council decides to build a new and bigger sewage treatment plant.

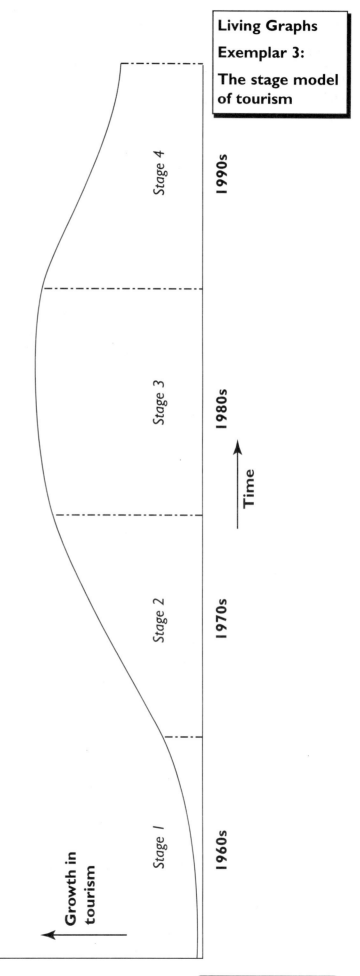

Living Graphs: Adapting the strategy

It was pointed out in the rationale that this is one of the easiest strategies to adapt to other contexts. Almost any line graph can be subjected to the treatment. Putting people in the statements (saying or doing things) helps the lower achieving pupils to get started. However, including some more generalised statements such as *'There are more Golden Weddings'* helps to differentiate for the more able pupils. Another angle that helps to generate statements is to use headings such as cause, effect, problem and solution.

> *Notice how important these headings were in the* Traffic Management Odd One Out *exemplar (see page 14).*

Within the ***Thinking Through Geography*** group other examples have been generated for:

- the change in North Sea fish stocks;
- climate graphs for a variety of locations;
- changes in the number of tractors on British farms;
- flood hydrographs;
- daily traffic flow on a busy urban road.

Afterthoughts

This strategy is a steady runner. It is easy to prepare, introduce, manage and follow-up. Pupils tend to like it and colleagues can take it up without much trouble or resistance. It makes pupils think and get behind the abstract lines on graphs thus connecting with reality. It can lead to some interesting insights into interpreting graphs and cause and effect. It is not the most spectacular strategy in terms of developing metacognition or transfer of learning, but the lack of risk involved recommends it as an excellent strategy to start curriculum development.

Mind Movies

Rationale

One of the basic tenets of teaching is that you should *start where children are at*. Actually this is really hard to do, because the pupils probably don't know where they are at, so how are you going to discover it! However, if you can get them to use their existing knowledge of topics, then it is far more likely that they will develop a personal understanding that will be remembered.

> *This paragraph relates very strongly to constructivism (see page 157).*

Mind movies are a brilliant way of accessing children's knowledge. It has to be said from the start that **Mind Movies** represent the most risky strategy in this book, because you have to persuade pupils to take their own knowledge seriously and to take themselves seriously. Your relationship therefore is crucial and mutual respect is required. To some extent it is a good test of pupils' attitudes to learning. Some low achieving pupils will smirk and giggle, perhaps because they do not consider that they might know something worth using. They can be worried about what they look like because 'image' is very important to them. Some high achieving pupils will not take it seriously and perhaps see it as beneath them. 'Learning is being told things and reading things' might summarise their approach to learning. In contrast, **Mind Movies** are quick, very motivating, fascinating to the teacher, highly flexible and if they don't work you can just move on with no damage done.

> *The bigger the contrast between a new activity like Mind Movies and 'normal' lessons, the greater the potential risk.*

Geography teaching proceeds as if memory of the written page is the most important source of remembering, but visual memory is very powerful, and especially valuable for low achieving pupils. It should be exploited. A grade F candidate sitting a GCSE paper may not be able to remember what was written on the case study pages of their text book or exercise book, but they may be able to remember powerful visual images that they used as a resource to answer questions. **Mind Movies** start the process of developing visual memory skills.

> *This is an example of trying to appeal to a wider selection of the senses (see page 162).*

Mind Movies Exemplar 1: The Kobe earthquake

Context

This example is suitable for use at both KS3 and 4, but it was trialled with several, setted Y9 classes. The top set class gave me most cause for concern, as they are lively and inclined to shout each other down, rather than listen and then respond! They are enthusiastic and competitive, but my relationship is very good with them. The bottom set are more passive.

The activity was used three-quarters of the way through a unit of work on Japan. Previous lessons had included a study of housing conditions in large cities such as Tokyo, as well as transport, industrial location and the physical geography of Japan (PoS paragraph 5a). Pupils had previous knowledge of plate tectonics and the causes of volcanoes and earthquakes from a module on natural hazards in Y8. Inevitably, as will be seen, they also had previous knowledge from the media.

Preparation

Very little physical preparation is needed.

More than any other strategy in this book *Mind Movies* depend on getting pupils to suspend disbelief and engage their imaginations, so it is extremely important to make up a story (the more dramatic the better) with lots of descriptive adjectives and planned dramatic pauses. You must avoid being too dead pan, but don't be over the top. Practice reading out the script, so that you are familiar with it and do not stumble over the words in class, as this can badly affect the atmosphere. I took the script in with me, written out with double spacing to make it easier to refer to (MIND MOVIES RESOURCE SHEET 1).

As a final point, avoid days when there are obvious distractions, like window cleaners, snow, or very strong winds.

Launching

Pupils need to be relatively *calm* for this exercise to work. You can tell them a bit about dreams to help persuade them, eg, *'Psychologists see dreams as very important because they tell us a great deal about what we know and feel about events and people. There is so much more in our minds than we are aware of: things that we have learned and remembered—otherwise it would not be in there. Our minds are a store of knowledge. In this lesson we are going to unlock and use some of the stored knowledge that you have. You have knowledge about earthquakes and I want to use it and I am going to use a tool called a mind movie to get it out. OK? Are you with me on this? I'm a psychologist right?'*

If you feel brave, try telling them about one of your dreams.

With this introduction you have a good chance when you ask them to close their eyes. Consider also switching off lights and closing curtains/blinds to reduce distractions.

Instructions

1. Ask pupils to close their eyes. If you get some people looking around tell them to cross their arms and put their heads down. It can help to play some soothing music to give them something to listen to, as some pupils are not used to silence.

2. When you have basic silence tell them that you are going to read them a real life account of someone caught in an earthquake and you want them to imagine this (ie, create a picture in their heads).

3. Start reading. This creates a scenario or starting point for their imagination.

4. After you finish, don't hesitate, but tell them immediately to keep their eyes shut and keep the movie running in their heads for a minute. *What happens next?*

[This is another example of bridging in—using other contexts to provide tolerance and a rationale. It also invites metacognitive awareness (see pages 159 and 162).]

This whole process is an excellent test of one's management skills—but inexperienced teachers should not feel disqualified as this teacher was an NQT.

Managing the activity

Although the activity lasts only a few minutes, it requires considerable professional skill. It is vital to have pupils' cooperation and trust, and the bit about psychologists and dreams may be very important in encouraging them to engage.

If you get total refusal from many pupils, cut your losses and move on. More likely you will have a few who are embarrassed or silly and inclined to titter. Quell them quietly, eg, *'Sssh Mark'*, while putting your head down or a finger pointing downwards; a shouting match will break the spell. Once you have read your scene-setting story and you have asked them to run the mind movie, then you should stay as quiet as possible: don't interrupt and maybe just walk quietly around (the quiet rhythm of footsteps can be helpful).

The top set were quiet for much longer than a minute and the bottom set managed the minute—just!

Follow-up

Any pupil who has done what was asked now has something to say—they cannot be wrong, only misguided! It is a shame if they cannot tell someone, so start by assigning them to pairs and giving the first person 2 minutes to describe what they *'saw'*. The second person has to take notes—this helps them focus. After 2 minutes, they swap. Following this they have to write down one thing that:

1. was similar between the two accounts;
2. was different between the two accounts;
3. they found surprising about the other account.

The bottom set found this much more difficult.

Ask for some feedback specifically on 1, 2 and 3. (This avoids pupils rambling and retelling the whole movie.) Encourage pupils to comment on or question the input of others, but try to avoid criticism of each other. On the board gradually accumulate generally agreed statements about what would happen and put them in time sequence.

Pupils now had to write, in their exercise books, their own account of what would happen. They wrote at much greater length than they would have done in other circumstances, especially the bottom set. The quality of writing was pleasing, although one disappointing feature was that some descriptions clearly related to their English homes in an earthquake (some others did set the scene in a Japanese home). I felt that I had a missed a drafting stage in the writing, where a bit of collaboration and checking could have greatly reduced this problem. All groups thoroughly enjoyed the lesson and asked to do mind movies again. Strangely they felt that they had not done any work, despite my protestations. This is a bit worrying and needs some thought.

Debriefing

Despite not seeing it as work, the pupils had achieved something very fundamental. They had used their existing knowledge as a starting point for an activity.

I asked them whether they could use **Mind Movies** in other subjects and they immediately saw the possibilities in history, where they were aware of the need to empathise and to put themselves in other people's shoes. They thought it was a useful technique, which did indeed bring out their existing thoughts and images. They made many suggestions about where their ideas had come from... films, magazines, videos in geography lessons and pictures in books. One girl had a father who had worked in Japan for a while. Pupils did not think however that they would be able to use the strategy for actively remembering for exams. There is some work to do here, *but I think that they are wrong.*

Mind Movies Exemplar 1: The Kobe earthquake

This is a simple form of writing frame (see page 81).

The social context is a factor here—one is trying to build a co-operative learning environment (see page 160).

This demonstrates the power of socialisation.

Another example of transfer (see page 162).

Mind Movies Exemplar 1: The Kobe earthquake

The earthquake script

You are in bed on your futon... fast asleep. Suddenly the floor turns to jelly, but this is no gentle liquid motion, but a jarring, wrenching, shuddering feeling of awesome proportions. Without warning the room has turned into a sickening roller coaster ride and it is terrifying.

The most frightening part is the sound. This is not a dull rumble like thunder. This is a deafening, roaring sound coming from everywhere... it sounds like the end of the world. Other sounds break in: books toppling off shelves, glasses, plates and windows shattering, and the television thumping to the ground and the screen shattering.

You realise that the horrendous creaking all around you is the building you live in. Walls, ceilings and floors look as if they are breathing in and out. Everything is rattling and shaking. You realise that there are 6 storeys of other apartments right above your head. The lights go off and it is pitch dark.

What happens next...?

> **Mind Movies Exemplar 2:**
>
> **A local nuclear power station disaster**

Context

This was used with a high ability Y9 class during a unit on man made natural disasters (PoS paras 15c and 15e). The previous lesson had been spent looking at the case study of Chernobyl and the effects of high level radiation on land and humans.

Most other headings are adequately covered by the first exemplar, except for the following:

Instructions

The class had done a *Mind Movie* before, so the instructions were easier to give. Exemplar 1 gives general instructions.

After the reading of the script, the specific instruction for this *Mind Movie* was:

> 'Keep your eyes shut. What are your first thoughts? Then start to think about what you will take in your bag and what your parent(s) should take.'

Follow-up

With this exemplar there is not quite the same excitement as the earthquake one, which could be a good thing. I allowed them 5 minutes to discuss in pairs their reactions and what might go in the bags. Following this they had to write down one thing that:

1. was similar between the two bags;
2. was different between the two bags;
3. they found surprising about the other bag;
4. would be different in the adults' bags.

> *A writing frame.*

I gave them only about 3 minutes to do this, after which we listened to a sample of answers.

I then asked them to produce written answers to the following two questions:

1. Remembering that you might not be able to return, make a list of just six things you have to take—give a reason for each.
2. Think about your life and that of your family and neighbours. What will the authorities need to do to take care of you?

Debriefing

This was not fully developed because of time. I concentrated on question 2. There was an excellent range of issues such as schools, housing, jobs, clothes, social activities, money and pets! We listed these on the board. I then asked them to consider how these things could be dealt with (a) in the short term and (b) in the long term. This needed more time, but it was a good start to considering a framework for understanding effects. For example, they thought that they could be taught in temporary classrooms at first, but in time new schools would be needed. Also they could be given money for a few weeks, but new jobs would need to be created in the longer term.

> *Effects is one of the big concepts elaborated through* Thinking Through Geography *(see page 168). Linkage could be made to the earthquakes exemplar as another example of bridging.*

Mind Movies Exemplar 2:

A local nuclear power station disaster

The nuclear disaster script

Imagine that you are sitting on your bed at home, listening to the local radio station. Look around the room and see what's there. Relax.

An urgent voice on the radio says:

This programme is interrupted for an important news bulletin.... At 4:00 p.m. a sequence of events at Hartlepool Power Station [insert the name of your nearest nuclear station] *led to the meltdown and explosion of the main reactor. Dangerous levels of radiation have been released into the atmosphere.*

The Department of the Environment and the Department of Health have declared a 30-kilometre evacuation zone. This includes the towns of Hartlepool, Middlesborough and Sunderland. Gateshead and South Shields will also be evacuated. Coaches will be at the end of each street starting in one hour. The police will begin clearing houses in 45 minutes. Please be ready to leave your homes. Each person will be allowed one small bag— and no more.

I repeat: a nuclear alert at Hartlepool means that your homes will have to be evacuated. Coaches will have to leave in one hour. This ends the news bulletin, programmes have been suspended until further notice.

Context

The class who trialled this were an able Y10 GCSE group, but that still includes students who will probably get Grade E. The unit of work was on residential environments. They are used to doing 'different' things and had done *Mind Movies* before, although this was a variation.

Preparation

There are two important points to the preparation: firstly, you must be familiar with the text and be able to read it fluently and with meaning; secondly (and more importantly), you must believe that this approach is valuable, through motivating students, assisting their understanding, or helping them to learn to remember. You may wish to duplicate the text for the class, but I prefer not to because it could undermine the message that they must actively use their own mental images.

Launching

I told the students that they had to listen very carefully to something that I was going to read them. (In terms of the floating analogy (on page 4) this class was highly receptive to doing challenging activities and thinking about their work, as a result of a lot of groundwork achieved by doing many of the activities in this book.)

Instructions

I told the class that the piece was quite long and therefore needed concentration. As I read it they should jot down any passages that would make good movie shots—the passages that are very visual and can create a picture. I gave them warning that eventually they would have to narrow it down to about 10 shots and suggest sound effects or music. They were very eager for me to start.

In order to make sure that this was clear I said that I would start reading and that they should stop me as soon as there was a suitable shot. I only got as far as '... *along the concrete walkway and I pick my way...*', and the hands shot up and they squealed 'Miss'.

Managing the activity

The obvious point to emphasise is that they should listen like never before. But further bear in mind the following points:

- Be prepared to stop reading for a few seconds to allow them to make some notes, but don't pause for too long;
- As they are bound to talk to each other because they are stimulated (and it helps them to process the words) be prepared to read over a little talk.

Debriefing

It was nice to go straight into some debriefing rather than written work. I asked first of all for their suggestions for good shots. (In MIND MOVIES RESOURCE SHEET 3, the underlined passages are generally those identified by the students.) There was a high level of agreement. They felt that all the movie shots were a bit grim and one boy suggested that they should be in black and white. Their suggestions for music centred around words like spooky, scary, slow. Most of the bands that they mentioned did not register with me.

I asked what they thought made some passages good for creating mental pictures. They suggested '*descriptive*', '*lots of adjectives*' and '*places*'. I suggested to them that these were the images that the author was trying to convey, communicate or portray to the reader. I also asked them whether they had remembered as much

---

Mind Movies Exemplar 3: Down and out in Sunderland?

You might like to consider the similarity between this and the launching for the Industrial Change in South Wales *exemplar (next section). This is after all partly a clarifying activity.*

Mind Movies Exemplar 3: Down and out in Sunderland?

This is another insight for them into metacognition (see page 159).

about what people had said in the piece. They said *'No'*—they were listening out for scenes and paid less attention to the 'talking parts'. I rounded this off by saying that if you decide to listen or read for a certain aspect in a text or spoken message it can help what you can pick out.

We spent some time talking about the view expressed by the people from Sunderland that it was a great place and they did not want to leave. The students' opinion was split—some felt that community was important while others felt that getting a job was paramount and that it was daft to stay in a rundown bit of Sunderland.

My last point was that the images and stories were a good way to remember facts for exams, as long as you were careful to read and answer the questions set. I had a fear that students might just relate the stories.

Follow-up

I asked them to choose 3 'shots', one to represent the causes of the poverty, one for the effects and the last for the action being taken to reduce the problems in high rise estates. I asked them to describe these shots in no more than 50 words with an appropriate label. A number of students asked if they could draw the shots and as I could see no objection I said *'Yes'*.

* * * * * *

Mind Movies: Adapting the strategy

Mind Movies should not be overused. Once or twice a term would be plenty. There is on-going pre-preparation that consists of finding good stories in the newspapers, magazines or novels, or bits of video of TV programmes, ready for the day when you need them.

We are considering trying to get students to revise some of their work for the GCSE exams by using visual memory, although it will be important to emphasise that the image has to be used carefully—as an aid to memory and understanding that needs to be consulted, and not an image to be described regardless of the question.

Afterthoughts

Mind Movies are something of a touchstone in relation to students' learning. Most students enjoy them, but it takes a lot of time and effort for them to accept that they are 'work' or learning. This could be the case with some fellow teachers—to say nothing of politicians.

The urban deprivation script

Nicci Gerrard visits Sunderland, home to single mums, pale pink sausages... and the Venerable Bede (from the Observer Review, 15 September 1996).

Mind Movies Exemplar 3: Down and out in Sunderland?

'Poor? You're talking about poor? Come in lass, you canna get more poor than this.' Ronald beckons me along the concrete walkway, and I pick my way over drifting piles of sodden newspapers that give off the dense ammonia tang of urine, half-empty tins of dog food, bits of charred wood, screwed up plastic bags, vast and sinister lumps of hair, shards of broken glass, cigarette packs, empty bottles, excrement that may be animal or human, heaps of rotting rubbish, into his flat. 'Poor, eh?' he says, as I stare around me trying to keep my face bland. 'Poor,' I agree.

Sunderland SR1/2 (postcode) stands alongside the docks, once thriving, now deserted: giant yellow and green cranes hang their motionless cables over a rubble of disused machinery. Assessed as the poorest district of Britain, it is an odd amalgam of trim new houses, low and net-curtained, that have been landscaped into neat estates with a fine view of the sea, and large bleak estates that stand in their own wasteland. These 'garths' (from the Old Norse *gardr* and the German *Garten*) are symbols of Sunderland's acute poverty; one by one they are being pulled down but in some flats curtains are still hanging where a window no longer exists. Ronald is the last resident of his garth: all the rest have been moved, but because he is behind with his rent, and because he is disgusted with the place they are offering him, he has stayed put with his 18 year-old daughter, Ann.

With every window and door in the large, red-bricked estate boarded up: some of the flats have been set fire to; in the courtyard where a cold wind slices in from the sea, bits of litter fly about like frantic seabirds and lumps of wood and masonry are scattered everywhere, as if the condemned building is shedding its dirty skin. Inside the dark flat, there are heaps of dirty sheets and clothes, teetering piles of encrusted dishes.

'That needs throwing away,' says Ronald fastidiously, picking up a tin of dogfood (though he has no dog) and putting it on the floor, among the bottles full of water:

Continued...

Mind Movies Exemplar 3: Down and out in Sunderland?

they've turned his gas off, and he's worried they will turn his water off next. The windows in the front are all smashed. He and Ann sleep in the same room, now, and listen in the dark to gangs of vandals roaming round the estate.

Ronald is a small man with a large belly. He used to be a shipyard worker, and then a parcel porter on the railways; now he's unemployed. 'What do I do with my days? Basically I sit here'—he points at a low stool on the kitchen floor—'and either face this way and watch the telly'—he points at the TV on one kitchen unit—'or I face that way and listen to the wireless. Or I go to the pub.' He smiles in a blank kind of way. 'I'm definitely fed up.'

Ann is standing on the walkway with a group of friends. All are unemployed; some have been on unemployment schemes. They are courteous, articulate. 'I'm not really bothered about working,' says Ann. 'It's not worth it. I've been on schemes, but they just pay £10 more than the dole. And the wages round here are so low you're better off with the dole.'

'Right,' says John. 'I was working 72 hours a week, for £2 an hour. I mean, that's not right. Living to work.'

'All you're doing is living to work,' says David. 'I get more from the Social.'

'I'd like to work,' says John. 'I want a decent life. I used to shoplift, and I'm trying to get away from all of that. Half the people are doing crime round here—give them a chance and they'd take it.'

'But I like Sunderland', says Ann. 'I wouldn't go anywhere else. London? Nah.' She stands nonchalantly on her foul walkway, in the dirty wind. 'I prefer it here. Sunderland's great, a great place to be. The people are great: they really care.'

I go back to Ronald's garth in the evening. It's dark and wind whistles up the stairways. I can make out some figures high up, cigarettes glowing. I can't believe anyone lives up there, alone, in the jagged malodorous ruin.

Most people who live in Sunderland love it with a fierce and patriotic ardour, and almost all insisted that they would never want to leave. Sharon, a single mother with two daughters and £23 a week after bills, says life might be a

Continued...

Mind Movies Exemplar 3: Down and out in Sunderland?

struggle, and her flat—three floors up, higgledy-piggledy with toys that she saves up for through the year and buys each Christmas, stuffy with cigarette smoke (everyone seems to smoke: these are the people Edwina Currie told to give up smoking and improve their diet) and heat from the bar fire—might be rather small. 'But I like it here. I know everybody. My sister lives across the way. And my mum.' She stares at the television flickering in the corner. 'What would I like to do in the future?' She shrugs her skinny shoulders and smiles quite cheerfully. 'Dunno. I don't really want to work, unless they pay more than the dole. I've never really been interested in a job. I never thought I'd get one. We're all unemployed round here. But we look out for each other. And I've got my bairns.'

'I would never leave here', says blue-eyed and beautiful Alison, another unemployed single mother who lives in a poky flat in a condemned building—a huge red-brick structure, round a huge ungreen courtyard where children play loudly. 'I don't have a job. It's hard, but we help each other out. The bairns love it here. Most of us have our families here too. I've always lived round here. Except on holidays—then we go to a caravan site 30 minutes away. I'd not change with the rich people in London, not for one day, not for one hour. They don't know the meaning of life.'

'The people round here' says the Salvation Army's bristle-headed Captain Malcolm Doyle 'are really kind. They are a loving community.' Doyle runs a hostel in the heart of the poorest area and sees signs of hope.

'Sunderland's future should be bright because its people are willing workers. But all this rebuilding doesn't solve the long-term unemployment—and we're in a generation now that's never known work.'

Along narrow roads, past the Prospect Row Mission House, all boarded up, past the empty warehouses, past isolated shops selling pale pink sausages and dusty cans of beans, past the working men's club called 'Cheers', sad and shut, past the city's motto mosaic—*nil desperandum*. Into the pub, the East Enders, where eight people in duffle coats sit staring into their drinks and the jukebox plays something jaunty. 'Yes, I've always lived here,' says a woman with silver hair and a puckered chin. 'No, it's very nice, thank you. Is it so very poor, dear? I didn't know. Everywhere's poor now, isn't it? Things are changing.'

Continued...

Mind Movies Exemplar 3: Down and out in Sunderland?

<u>Into another pub. It is rumoured to be the East End's drug centre, and is full of younger people playing snooker, smoking and drinking their slow time away. At one table a group of men play dominoes and they ask if I want to join in. So I sit on a broken sofa, click a few spotted pieces into line.</u> They used to work in the shipyards but haven't had a job for a decade. A man with small ears and a sweet smile tells me that it's hard not to be a breadwinner, but that's how life is. You can't get angry, can you? It's nobody's fault, is it? Click, click through the evening, and the beer sinks in the tankard and the cigarettes are sucked to the filter: a way of truly killing time. 'Why should we look for work? There isn't any, except for work that pays so little it's not worth it. Who wants to earn £1.70 an hour? We'll never work again will we?'

The Venerable Bede lived in Sunderland and great industrialists (Isambard Kingdom Brunel, Joseph Swann, William Hudson) came here. Industry flourished in the town, and the town nearly died when that industry left. But now Sunderland is home to the Nissan factory; it has been made into a city; its football team has made it into the Premier League. Some think that the future looks good. The people I met in the East End were neither obsessed with their past, nor much concerned with their future. They were living implacably in the present, one foot in front of the other, one cigarette, one pint of beer, one conversation, one more day gone by. And it seemed a kind of way to be happy.

END

Mysteries

Rationale

Mysteries are probably the most powerful strategy in this book—they can completely transform the teaching and learning process. Pupils are given 16-30 pieces of information on individual pieces of paper and they produce an answer to a central question. The *Mysteries* are designed to encourage pupils to deal with ambiguity through addressing a question which has no single correct answer and where they are not even sure what information is relevant—rather like real life in fact. In the process they have to practise and develop some crucial skills:

* sorting relevant information from irrelevant information;
* interpreting information;
* making links between disparate pieces of information;
* speculating to form hypotheses;
* checking and refining;
* explaining.

Mysteries have a high level of challenge (see page 159).

These are fundamental problem-solving skills.

Far too frequently pupils are given written tasks in which they have a page of text and all they have to do is retrieve the right words from the page to complete the task. There is little challenge in this and learning skills are not developed to any significant extent: they just learn how to perform a ritual. This is not how problems and issues present themselves in higher education or real life problem solving. In these contexts you have to take discrete, apparently unconnected pieces of information and fit them together to make sense of disorder, read between the lines, come up with a variety of ideas and evaluate them. This strategy mirrors these situations far more closely. It is fundamental to the *Mystery* that the information is presented 'semi-digested' and that it is presented on pieces of paper that can be physically manipulated. We have observed on numerous occasions that pupils will change their minds as they move pieces of paper around—the moving actually helps them think.

This relates to the Vygotskyan idea of a ZPD—physically doing something with others may be important in learning how to do it mentally.

Ultimately the pupils should write detailed and thoughtful explanations in relation to the central question; thus they are given an opportunity not only to present evidence in relation to NC levels, but also to develop the skills to improve their achievement in relation to those levels. (The writers of the book contributed the mystery centred on the Kobe earthquake to the SCAA publication *Optional Tasks and Tests* for teacher assessment at KS3.) *Mysteries* are a fantastic tool for developing teachers' skills in diagnostic and formative assessment, through watching groups handle information, listening to their talk and finally reading the written product.

The successful completion of *Mysteries* depends on co-operative group work in which productive learning and social relationships are fostered. Inevitably disagreement may emerge as group members want to do it their own way. This is particularly true of older and more able pupils who are more confident of their opinions (even opinionated). If handled sensitively though (and with patience!), pupils can develop speaking and listening skills and learn ways in which group conflicts can be resolved.

The Philosophy for Children programme explicitly seeks to create a community of enquiry.

The main concepts addressed by *Mysteries* are cause and effect, but the concept of classification underpins the pupils' mystery solving strategies. Furthermore, some *Mysteries* (through their content) begin to unpack other concepts, such as decision making and systems.

Mysteries Exemplar 1: Industrial change in South Wales

Context

This ***Mystery*** was designed to be used as part of a KS3 scheme of work on economic activities (para 13c) and was carried out with a Y8 mixed ability group, who were demanding at the best of times. They were not unmotivated, but they were somewhat immature and restless, prone to seek reassurance at every turn. The activity seeks to highlight some of the economic, social and environmental issues associated with industrial change in developed economies, whilst providing timely reinforcement of industrial location factors.

The pupils had covered some introductory work on employment structures and were to cover examples of primary, secondary and tertiary industry. The activity could, just as easily, be included in a GCSE unit on economic geography.

Preparation

Several things need to be done to give the activity the best chance of running smoothly.

1. Decide on the composition of groups. We would recommend 3: in larger groups pupils have a problem in seeing the information in front of them and loafers can hide. We would also recommend fairly mixed ability groups, so that the more able and better group workers are spread out, within the constraints set by personalities. Your professional skills are crucial here.

2. Cut the statements up and put them into envelopes, one per group (MYSTERIES RESOURCE SHEET 1).

3. Put the key question on the front of each envelope (see Instructions).

4. Decide on further support material and organise it so that each group has it available (MYSTERIES RESOURCE SHEETS 2 and 3, which provide some maps). The importance of this material varies from class to class. The resource material can be used at 3 levels:
   (i) as the basis of some comprehension exercises to highlight information about industrial decline;
   (ii) as the basis of a class discussion to the same end; or
   (iii) just given out to pupils so that they can consult it if they want to (more probable with more able groups).

5. Think about the room and the space available. Each group needs a fair amount of working space to spread out their bits of paper. You may need to consider moving furniture.

The line graph of coal production could be used for a Living Graph exercise.

Launching

Certain expectations need to be worked on, as ***Mysteries*** break most of the rules about the type of work that pupils are given. Assuming that this is the first ***Mystery*** you do with a class (as it was with this Y8 group), we offer the following:

Now nearly everyone has seen one of those TV programmes with police detectives solving murders—Inspector Morse, Taggart, A Touch of Frost, Cracker. OK? In these programmes, the detective is trying to solve a mystery, usually a murder or some other crime. They have clues or pieces of evidence from witnesses or from forensic evidence—the bullet from the gun, footprints, skin from the murderer found under the nails of the victim, a button on the floor, a fingerprint, the victim's recent history, a blue hatchback seen near the scene. They take these clues and try to work out who the murderer was, by forming theories and then checking out whether they are correct. They have to work hard and they have to think. You have got a mystery to solve today—not a murder, but something to do with geography—where you have got to use the same sort of skills as

Another example of bridging into an activity (see page 162).

the detective. You have got to work things out, form theories, discuss them, and see if they make sense.'

Of course you have to make sure that the word 'theory' makes sense to pupils. Deal with those who want to include Hercule Poirot, Miss Marple, Inspector Dalgleish, etc, in your list of detectives, those who want to tell you about DNA, and so on. Get them used to the idea that in this ***Mystery*** (unlike the TV detectives) there is no one correct answer. You want to hear their explanation; you want to hear which information they think is relevant (or not); and how they have linked it together to make a whole, sensible, convincing explanation. Like the fictional detectives on TV, they have to sort through a lot of confusing information, they go up dead ends in their investigations and they have to use inspired guesswork. Tell them that they may have to give their explanation to the rest of the class.

Finally, the envelopes can help; they can create a sense of intrigue and curiosity, even when you have used them before. It is a signal that they will have to think, speak, and work hard as a group and (although they may groan) secretly most pupils really enjoy the challenge.

Mysteries Exemplar 1: Industrial change in South Wales

Instructions

As ***Mysteries*** are different and go against the flow, it is important to give clear instructions. The following is offered as a guide only. Your professional skills, teaching style and knowledge of pupils will influence your decisions here.

1. Organise the groups.
2. Distribute the envelopes plus any additional resources.
3. Ask the pupils to read the key question on the envelope without opening it and ask them to make some predictions about what the answer might be. The key question is **'Why is Dai Williams involved in the building of a new Japanese restaurant in Bridgend?'**
4. Tell them to open the envelope and spread out the statements so that everyone can see (a crucial moment—if you have deviants they may take the opportunity to blow all the paper over the floor). Ask them to read the statements quickly to see if there are any words that need explaining and to check that they have a full set of statements. Give them 3-5 minutes to read and then ask if they have any questions about the information.
5. Get them to find on the map(s) all the places and things mentioned on the cards.
6. Explain that as a group they are going to use the statements to come up with an answer to the key question. Stress the following points (again):
   * that they need to consider all the information carefully and produce a full explanation, but that not all the information is relevant;
   * that there is not a right order or a right answer;
   * that they can use any other information that they have (like general knowledge) to put together the most convincing explanation (you can make reference back to fictional detectives).
7. Tell them that sorting the statements is important and will help them, but don't suggest too much about how they should do this.
8. Explain that they need to keep checking back to the statements that are discarded to see if they can be fitted into the explanation at any point— the more detail the better. Stress the need to keep looking at the links between the statements as some help to explain or clarify others.

The ambiguity is deliberate—the pupils have to learn the necessity of clarifying tasks and problems and information.

They are encouraged to use their general knowledge.

There is a temptation to over-instruct, but they will not listen beyond a certain point, so you will have to be prepared to repeat all these points to individual groups.

Mysteries Exemplar 1: Industrial change in South Wales

An example of scaffolding.

This experience amply demonstrates the vital importance of classifying skills (see page 113).

Managing the activity

One of the reasons for including this as the lead exemplar is that it was the first time that this group had done a *Mystery*. It did not go perfectly. It takes time and practice for some pupils to get the hang of doing *Mysteries* and even then some struggle. The whole point is that they are **learning important skills** which do not come automatically.

A couple of groups were somewhat overwhelmed by the information and I had to spend much of my time supporting them. One of the groups had only 2 members, because one of the brightest boys was away. If he had been there the problems would have been eased with that group. The best way of helping them was to pull out one statement such as *'In 1973 Sony opened its factory at Bridgend. Staff were brought over from Japan to manage the company,'* but first making sure they understood that Sony is a Japanese company. Then I asked them to find another statement that was about Sony— *'Sony's 1400 employees are mostly women'*. I asked whether Sony employed men and they said *'No'*. I could not stay with them all the time, but I would periodically return and pull out another statement: *'Dai Williams left school to be an apprentice joiner down the pit in 1971. He has become very skilled in this job'*. I then asked them to find other statements about Dai or mines. They were working a little more confidently now. Sometimes they could see the links and sometimes they couldn't until I prompted them. It was slow progress and it felt like pulling teeth. It is only with hindsight that this exercise was helping me to diagnose their learning difficulties and their inability to categorise.

Talk is at the heart of this activity.

However, the majority of the groups were getting on much better. It was not an easy lesson to manage because the groups were constantly asking me questions and I was trying to keep an eye on the two struggling groups, but in the 15–20 minutes that they worked on the task initially there was a lot of productive talk. The following points should be useful pointers based on the experience of this lesson and more general experience of using *Mysteries*.

- Despite all that you might say, groups tend to look for a simple correct answer and they discard too much information. In this case the better groups worked out that Dai lost his job in the pits and was now working on the building of a Japanese restaurant started up for Japanese managers and their families. But they did not stop to think why Sony had located in South Wales, so they ignored the information about the M4 or land prices. Therefore you have to draw their attention to some statements and say *'Have you thought about this?'*— but do not do this too much. I like to refer back to the TV detectives and say that they have to find out as much as they can about *why* things happen, not just *what* happened.

- With groups new to *Mysteries*, try to praise and reinforce their efforts, whilst spurring them on. Also remember to keep an open mind to different interpretations and reasoning—there is no single correct answer to this *Mystery*.

This advice epitomises the change in teacher role in some phases of Thinking Through Geography activities.

- It is important with this activity to get the right balance between what is management and what could be deemed interference. It is obviously important to keep a close watch on how groups are working, whilst resisting the temptation to jump in too quickly. Many of the skills that are important in learning are forged in the heat of discussion. We would recommend that you DO NOT systematically visit groups heralding your arrival with *'How are you getting on'*. If groups are on task, leave them alone—visiting tends to disrupt discussion badly. Clearly this applies more strongly to older or more able groups.

- We would recommend carrying a notebook or piece of paper to note down some of what you overhear—to be called upon in the debriefing.

Spend as much time as you can just watching and listening. Interestingly you sometimes hear ideas that you think are good rejected by a group and you can use this later. Listening is invaluable, although it is unlikely that you will have much time when you use a *Mystery* for the first time.

- A model scenario would involve two 50-minute lessons: the first one being used for discussion and manipulation of information, and the second for the production of an individual extended piece of writing. It is extremely helpful if groups are given a chance to make some notes before the end of the first lesson, to capture some of their thinking so that they don't lose the trail before the next lesson. I have also tried getting them to make a 'map' of how they have grouped the statements, so that they can start from the same place next lesson.

- If you have a group or two who work very quickly, but perhaps superficially, and they resist your invitation to consider the relevance of other statements ask them to produce a time line for all the statements that have any mention or reference to time.

Mysteries Exemplar 1: Industrial change in South Wales

Differentiation by extension task.

Debriefing

Debriefing with this class was confined to asking for pupil's explanations as to why Mr Williams was working on building a Japanese restaurant. I asked a group which I knew had a simple explanation first and they explained that he used to work in the mines, but that he had lost his job and was now working as a builder. With a bit of probing about why it was a Japanese restaurant they added that the restaurant was for Japanese workers at the factory. At this point my eavesdropping did pay off because I knew that one group at least had considered why the mines had closed after I had shoved a couple of statements under their noses. There followed some further discussion (led by my questions) to clarify why the mines had closed and why this had encouraged Japanese companies to locate in South Wales. There was one boy in particular who was able to point out that there would have been a lot of workers available once the mines and steelworks had closed. Finally, I asked if any group could add any more to the explanation. One group offered an explanation about the importance of good roads and the building of the Severn Bridge, and another offered that, if so many Japanese could speak English, it would be easy to come to Wales to live. It was really only at this point (perhaps 15 minutes into the discussion) that I had the feeling they were really seeing the point of the exercise, because as a point was brought up by one group others would want to chip in. I asked if any pieces of information were of no use. After a pause someone said, *'the one about pollution'*. Then someone else said, *'the one about Sony being a multi-national'*. It then emerged that most had not understood what multi-national meant. I replied that they should have asked when they had the chance. Overall it was an encouraging discussion; it had begun to sink in that you could change your mind and go beyond your first idea. In the whole class discussion they had seriously begun to hypothesise.

This is a further illustration of the change demanded of pupils—they are being socialised into new learning roles.

Time did not allow for any consideration of how they had done the task. Therefore we offer below some general guidelines on how this could be started.

- Choose a group that you think will have a reasonable but perhaps unsophisticated and undeveloped explanation. (You will only know this if you have been listening.) Praise whatever they come up with, but follow up with a few supplementary probing questions: *'Can you expand on that part'* or *'Tell us more about....'* or *'Why do think that...?'*

- It is even more desirable to get other groups to do the probing but you may need to goad them into this role, eg, *'Has anybody got an alternative?'* This may flush out a group, but you can pressurise by

You want pupils to do some of the initiating (see page 160).

Mysteries Exemplar 1: Industrial change in South Wales

saying *'So, this is the best answer that we can come up with—everyone else agrees that their solution is not as good as this one'*. If you have taken notes in your eavesdropping you will be able to quote particular arguments or approaches that you have observed.

- The other important generic question is *'How did you do the task?'* Remember, this is the stage in the process when you can open up the possibility of learning about learning—and you may get blank looks. It is impossible here to describe all the responses you might get, and all the backup questions that you might have to ask: we can only give a lead. So try three lines of inquiry:

    (i) *What did you physically do with the pieces of paper and why?* This raises all sorts of important issues such as sorting relevant from irrelevant, how the statements have been grouped and perhaps also how they have been sequenced.

    (ii) *How did your ideas and approach change over the course of the discussion?* This raises issues such as refining ideas, rethinking and coming up with alternative ideas rather than just the first stab, checking and the need for more information.

    (iii) *How did your group operate?* This starts to unpack groupwork skills, so you may need to ask: *Who took the lead? Was it hard to get everyone to listen? Did everyone get a chance to contribute? How did you resolve disagreements?* You may even ask whether anyone was impressed by the thinking or approach of someone else.

This phase helps to develop metacognition (see page 159).

This may help in reducing impulsive behaviour.

Trigger and background factors

We would strongly recommend that if circumstances allow you set at least one more task. Introduce the terms 'trigger' and 'background factors'. Trigger factors are the immediate causes of an event or situation: they make it happen in a particular place at a particular time. Trigger factors tend to be episodic. Background factors are generally ever-present and more widespread, or endemic. They are less visible than trigger factors, but being endemic they predispose the event or situation. In geography they tend to be the physical, biological, socio-economic or political factors. The Braer tanker disaster in Shetland can be analysed in terms of trigger and background. The background factors were the poor maintenance of the vessel and training of the crew due to the competitive market in oil transport (socio-economic), the lack of a tug on standby (political), and the routing of vessels through sensitive marine environments rather then taking longer safer routes (economic). The trigger factors were the fierce storm (episodic and geographically localised) and the breakdown of the engine (bad luck and human error). It was an accident waiting to happen, it just needed a particular set of circumstances to trigger it.

Trigger and background are part of the vocabulary of causation (see page 167).

An example of bridging (see page 162).

So ask the pupils to group the statements that form part of their explanation into 2 piles: the trigger and the background. Allow them to have an in-between group if you are so inclined.

In debriefing this exercise, offer them an example from everyday life where trigger and background factors can be used to understand events. Make one up or perhaps use the following:

Another piece of bridging.

> *'Our family has just decided to buy a new car. We have been thinking about it for a long time now, because our car is nearly ten years old, it is a bit unreliable and it costs a fortune to have all the repairs done. Besides, no one in our street has got one that old and the kids say that they get teased about it; they say it is old fashioned. But it is difficult to raise the money.'* (all background)

'Just recently though a couple of things happened that just made up our minds. Firstly we got a new puppy, a Dalmatian, and you cannot have a dog that big in a saloon, so we decided that we had to get an estate car. Then last weekend, our neighbour, Frank, said that his brother-in-law was getting rid of a Sierra estate, only 4 years old, in really good condition, and that we could have it for what the garage had offered him when he gets his new one.' (triggers)

> **Mysteries Exemplar 1: Industrial change in South Wales**

You can follow this up by asking pupils for examples of events or decisions in their lives where trigger and background factors can be used to explain the pattern of causation. Do not be too disappointed if some pupils cannot apply this framework, or if those that do are vague, confused or wrong. This is an immensely powerful concept and it needs time to grow. Be delighted with any positive outcomes.

> *An example of encouraging transfer*

Follow-up

Writing up the task is important to consolidate what has been learned. The pupils were asked to write an answer to the initial question. It also provides a written product which reassures some pupils and meets many external requirements.

They started this at the end of the second lesson and had to complete it for homework. If I am honest, the results were disappointing: too many pupils just wrote down what they could remember was on the statements without much attempt to explain the original question. The quality of writing did not match the quality of discussion. I believe that I did not do enough to get them to structure their writing, but this disappointment does not negate the value of the small group and whole-class discussion.

> *This might be helped by the use of writing frames (see page 81).*

Mysteries Exemplar 1: Industrial change in South Wales

Statements—Industrial change

1.	In 1973, Sony opened its factory at Bridgend. Staff were brought from Japan to manage the company.
2.	Britain is a member of the EU.
3.	A golf course has opened on the site of an old spoil heap. Mr Ishiguro is a keen golfer.
4.	Megan Jones has started working as a remote control assembler at the new Sony factory.
5.	Dai Williams has started work for a building company which has just won a contract to convert a row of old miners cottages into a Japanese restaurant.
6.	Proposals were put forward in 1991 to open a second factory at a site in Pencoed, near Bridgend.
7.	The new Sony site is situated on the M4.
8.	The nearest mine at Maesteg closed down several years ago when the coal seam became exhausted.
9.	Many oil-fired power stations have been opened around the country.
10.	Dai Williams left school as an apprentice joiner down the local pit in 1971. He became very skilled in this job.
11.	During the mid 1980s competition from cheaper foreign imports meant that many Welsh mines could not sell their coal.
12.	Sony is a huge muti-national electronics company.
13.	Mining was the only job that Dai has ever done.

Continued...

Mysteries Exemplar 1: Industrial change in South Wales

14.	In 1973, Britain had the fastest growing demand for colour televisions.
15.	Mrs Ishiguro operates a food co-operative which distributes Japanese food to the local Japanese community.
16.	Sony's 1400 employees are mostly women.
17.	Land prices in South Wales are cheaper than in the South East of England.
18.	Many iron and steelworks in South Wales closed in the 1960s and 1970s.
19.	Sony doubled the factory size in 1982. By 1986 the factory was working 3 continuous shifts to increase output to keep up with demand.
20.	Machines have been introduced into the mines which can do the work of 20 men.
21.	Sony products will be sold throughout Europe.
22.	In 1976, the Welsh Development Agency began setting up industrial estates supplied with all the services needed by factories.
23.	English is the second language in all Japanese schools.
24.	In 1966, the Severn Bridge opened linking South Wales to England's motorway network.
25.	People are becoming increasingly concerned with reducing pollution to protect the environment.
26.	The M4 extends from Port Talbot to London.
27.	18.5% of all Japanese-owned industry in Britain is located in Wales.
28.	Megan Jones likes Japanese food.

Mysteries Resource Sheet 1

Mysteries Exemplar 1: Industrial change in South Wales

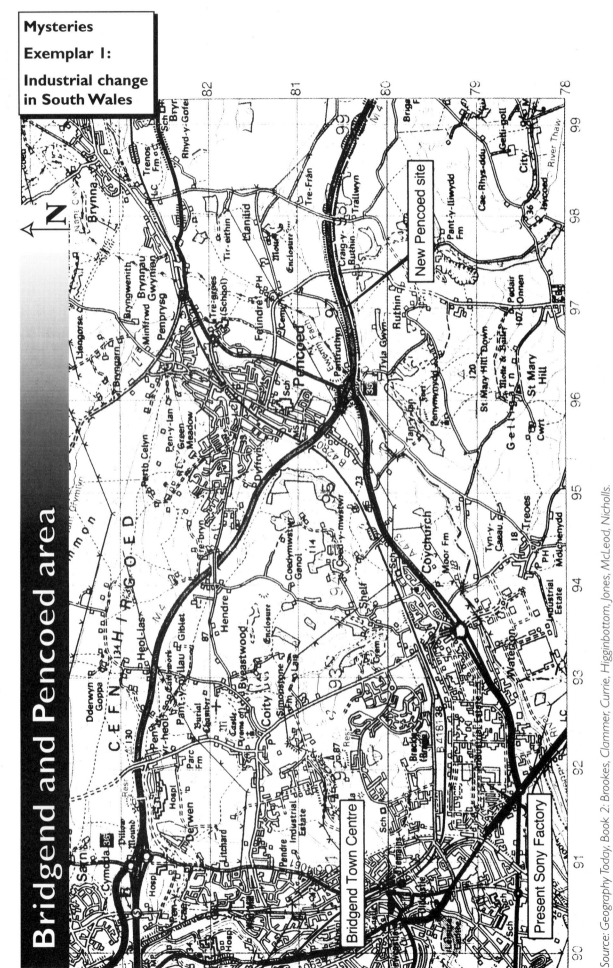

Bridgend and Pencoed area

Source: Geography Today, Book 2: Brookes, Clammer, Currie, Higginbottom, Jones, McLeod, Nicholls.

Mysteries Exemplar 1: Industrial change in South Wales

Heavy industry in the South Wales coalfield

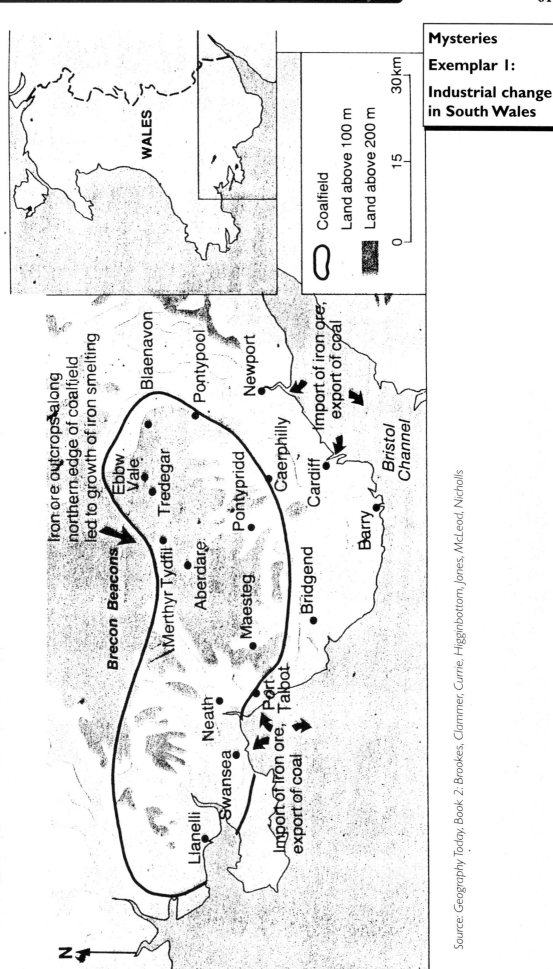

Source: Geography Today, Book 2: Brookes, Clammer, Currie, Higginbottom, Jones, McLeod, Nicholls

Mysteries Exemplar 1: Industrial change in South Wales

Coal exports from South Wales

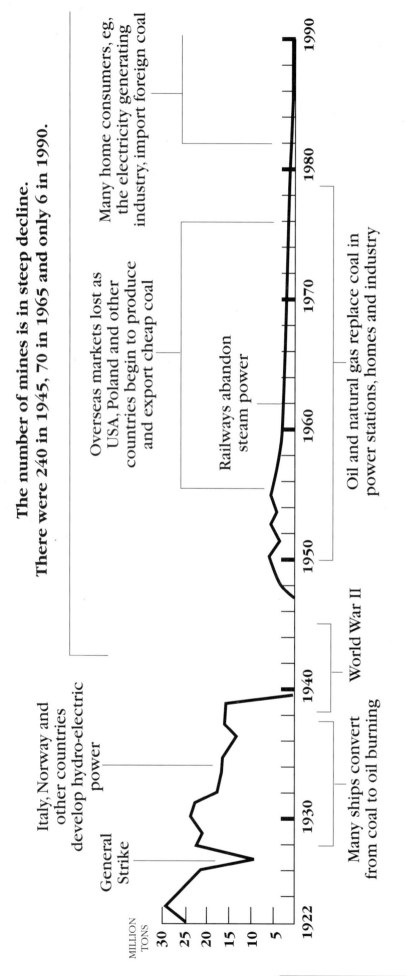

> Mysteries Exemplar 2:
> Who is to blame for Sharpe Point flats?

Context

This *Mystery* investigates the demise of the type of high rise block of flats commonly found in inner-city residential environments as a result of redevelopment in the 1960s and stimulates the students to consider who is to blame. It was used with a very mixed ability Y10 GCSE group which, given the catchment of the school, would have a lower average ability than most schools. Nonetheless, they were a well motivated and affable group, generally willing to work in groups and to try new activities. The class included one highly disruptive student, who would not participate in the activity (he worked separately in the department office).

The activity was used in the spring term in a unit on urban geography (NEAB Syllabus C). The class had already done some work on local residential environments—suburbs, inner-city terraces and outer-city council estates, but not on redevelopment. We feel that with virtually no change the same activity could be used with KS3 (para 12d) or with an A Level group.

The learning outcomes are numerous depending on the direction that the whole class discussion and follow-up takes, but typically will include:

- the characteristics and problems associated with high rise council blocks;
- some of the reasons for these problems;
- the hypothesis that change in urban areas affects different groups in different ways and therefore tends to generate conflict;
- an appreciation of the values held by different groups;
- an appreciation of some of the factors that affect planning decisions.

Preparation

The guidelines given for the first exemplar in this section apply here equally. However, each *Mystery* may need its own stimulus material. If your teaching already includes high rise blocks, you will have your own resources. This class had watched the (old, but still useful) BBC programme on *Inner Cities* which features the problems of high rise blocks in Glasgow. Also included is a report from the *Sun* newspaper, which can be used to get the students to speculate about living conditions in flats (see MYSTERIES RESOURCE SHEET 5).

Launching

I started with copies of a photo of a block of flats, which captured the students' attention and asked them, *'This looks like a perfectly good block of flats, so why are they blowing it up?'* I got a number of suggestions, generally along the right lines, ie, it was going to fall down anyway. I then asked if anyone lived or had lived in a block of flats. Fortunately one student had lived in a high rise block and volunteered that it was indeed horrible: the lifts did not work; it was incredibly windy; and the flat was cold. The only good things were the views and being able to watch large birds gliding past. On another occasion I would like to use the *Sun* cutting to raise questions about the lack of community that can prevail in tower blocks.

> *Students' knowledge being used, which others could relate to.*

Instructions

The instructions given for the first exemplar fit exactly for this one, but actually this group had done a *Mystery* before, so the instructions were more by way of reminders. They knew roughly what was expected. It was, however, important to stress the central question *'Who is to blame for Sharpe Point Flats?'* For a more able group you might prefer to extend the question to *'Why are the Sharpe Point Flats going to be demolished, and who is to blame?'*

Mysteries

Exemplar 2:

Who is to blame for Sharpe Point flats?

Managing the activity

Management follows the same lines as in the first exemplar, but this class had no groups who were overwhelmed. Therefore it was possible to do more listening to the groups. Nonetheless, it was necessary at certain points to push groups by asking them to consider whether a particular statement could be relevant to the causes (or blame) for the demolition.

Debriefing

Debriefing in this case was lengthy, but as often happens did not cover all the ground that was intended. The verbal explanations that groups offered were of a high quality. As is often the case, the first group came up with a simple explanation: *'it was the council's fault because they had not looked after the flats properly'*. But over the next 20 minutes we gradually added to that (as other groups offered more and I probed) with such questions as, *'Go on, tell us more?'* or *'Why was that?'* The builders got a lot of blame; some students started to blame the kids; but others defended them and said that they only misbehaved because they were bored. They started to draw parallels to their own estates. We returned to place the blame on the council generally, but there was also the view that you could not blame any one person or group.

Some instinctive transfer.

In my view, this was a sophisticated discussion from this group. I was really pleased that they had concluded that the world is shades of grey and not just black and white. At the same time I was slightly concerned that they would find shades of grey much harder to remember in an exam. I was not surprised that they did not unearth the part played by government in rushing ahead with large scale redevelopment without thinking of the communities involved or the untried technology. I think that an A Level group would have got into this.

This suggests that some pupils at least were using formal operational thinking (a Piagetian concept).

One other omission from the debriefing was not exploring how they had done the task.

Follow-up

As homework the class wrote an answer to the central question.

Another productive task would be to ask the students to identify the possible effects of the demolition of the flats. One could expect a range of issues to emerge: disruption of work and social lives; people living in temporary accommodation; better living conditions; the building of a local superstore; improved health, etc.

One could also ask the class to classify the reasons for the demolition of the flats into trigger and background factors.

Mysteries Exemplar 2:

Who is to blame for Sharpe Point flats?

MUM AND BABE IN DEATH DIVE

by MURIEL BURDEN

A TEENAGE mum hated by her neighbours killed herself and her baby by diving from the fifth floor of a block of flats yesterday.

Petite blonde Cara Jennings, 17, leapt out of a balcony window after finding herself locked out of her flat.

Tragic

The unpopular single mum and her month-old daughter crashed to the ground 80ft below—just feet from neighbour Norman Hines.

Pensioner Mr Hines said: "I heard an almighty thud. The baby landed near the girl and they were both covered in blood."

After the suicide plunge at Wordsworth House in Woolwich, South London, other tenants told why they despised tragic Cara.

Next-door neighbour Barbara Davidson, 20, said: "She had different men in at every hour of the day and night."

"Most people here disliked her. She wrote graffiti everywhere and was a trouble-maker."

Lorraine Davies said: "She wasn't responsible enough to look after the baby."

"She had more boyfriends than anyone I know. I'm sure she didn't know who the father was."

Source: 'The Sun', newspaper report.

Mysteries

Exemplar 2:

Who is to blame for Sharpe Point flats?

Statements—Sharpe Point

1.	The Environmental Health Officer has found that the heating pipes are lagged with asbestos.
2.	The Northern Housing Association has recently renovated 100 Victorian houses near the river.
3.	The tenants' association members refused to pay any rent unless the building is repaired and a security guard is put in the entrance at night.
4.	A group of new age travellers are squatting in Flat 38, one of 22 empty flats (out of 182).
5.	Steve and Claire McLean with their baby daughter were on the TV news when they camped outside the council offices in protest at being offered a flat in the block.
6.	Asbestos is known to cause cancer if it gets into people's lungs.
7.	The Walkers are the only people in the block who have bought their flat.
8.	When old Mr Clark died, he had been dead for eight days before anyone noticed. They could not get his coffin in the lift.
9.	Janet Dalton won't let Diane (8) and Richie (10) play outside after police found them sniffing glue at the bottom of the stair-well with older kids.
10.	Many people have been mugged and cars stolen and vandalised on the estate.
11.	When officially opened in 1969 by the Minister of Housing, Sharpe Point was praised for using new technology—steel frames and concrete panels. The flats were built in record time.
12.	The walls in the flats are very thin.
13.	Smith Fastbuild Ltd, the builders, went bankrupt in 1978 after a major scandal over faulty workmanship in pre-fabricated buildings.

Continued...

Mysteries Exemplar 2: Who is to blame for Sharpe Point flats?

14.	Over half the residents of the block are retired or unemployed.
15.	There are fantastic views over the city and along the river from the top floors.
16.	Mr and Mrs Walker have to replace their mouldy wallpaper every year.
17.	Cyril Beecham, 72, spends his evenings watching TV in his overcoat with an eiderdown over his legs to keep warm.
18.	Spike (12) and Baz (14) enjoy playing in the lifts.
19.	All council tenants have the right to buy their home from the council at a discount price.
20.	The estate in which the block is located has the worst health statistics in the city.
21.	The waiting list for council homes has about 1500 names on it.
22.	Proceeds from the sale of council flats and houses can be used to modernise and repair the council's remaining properties.
23.	Baz got a secondhand drum kit for his birthday. He practises with his mates when his mum is out at work behind the bar at The Boilermaker's Arms.
24.	The Boilermaker's Arms and St Justin's church are all that remain of the old days.
25.	Safebury's have been looking for a large inner-city site for a new supermarket and are prepared to contribute to the costs of site clearance.
26.	Mr Walker has a pigeon loft on his allotment, half a mile away.
27.	When the old terraces were pulled down in 1968, the community was scattered to new houses on several different outer-city council estates.
28.	Gary Payne, chairman of the Sharpe Point tenants' association, was elected to the council last May.

Mysteries Exemplar 3: The lost livestock of Loxley Coppice Farm

Systems is one of the big concepts (see pages 168–169).

Context

This ***Mystery*** was trialled with a Y12 A Level group. There were 9 in the group and they were not particularly able for such a group. About half contribute freely to class discussions using the opportunity to test opinions and float ideas. From their previous studies they had some knowledge of farm systems and case studies of hill sheep farms and arable farms. However they are very urban students with little personal experience of the countryside. They were following the ULEAC syllabus B (16-19 Project). The primary objective of the activity was to encourage further their ability and willingness to discuss ambiguous issues as a foundation for the decision making paper.

In planning the ***Mystery***, the following learning outcomes were targeted:

* an understanding of farms as systems with inputs, processes and outcomes;
* an understanding of some of the factors influencing farmers' decision making, particularly economic, political and personal values;
* an understanding of the impact of agriculture on natural systems and the landscape;
* an insight into the inconsistencies there may be in one's own attitudes.

As with all ***Mysteries*** cause and effect are central concepts but the content of this Mystery also puts systems at centre stage.

Preparation

Being topical, BSE was a perfect lead-in to this activity, as it connects so directly to systems analysis and the social, political and economic factors that affect farmers' decision making. BSE also clearly raises many moral and value-based issues. Therefore, I made sure that I was saturated in BSE news items. I also managed to borrow a toy Friesian cow from a small friend. I also had available Hart (1984) pages 16-19, for the photographs of agricultural landscapes.

The rest of the preparation was as in previous exemplars.

Launching

Another good example of students' knowledge being accessed to assist understanding.

I started the lesson by holding up the toy Friesian cow. It is amazing that even sixth-formers are hooked by such simple tricks. I pointed to the head and said *'Why am I pointing to the head of this cow?'* It took about 3 seconds for 2 students to blurt out *'BSE'*. I then asked everyone to write down 3 reasons for the outbreak of BSE, but added that they should think of the reasons that had been given by all the people concerned—farmers, vets, politicians, vegetarians, doctors—as they might have different angles in the 3 reasons. I gave them 2 minutes and asked for their reasons. I got plenty of response, but mainly around the theme of contaminated food and people ending up eating bits of brain and spinal chord because abattoirs were careless. I knew that I had at least two vegetarians in the class, so I asked them why they did not eat meat. One replied that it was not fair to eat animals, it was cruel. I asked whether BSE had anything to do with being cruel to animals and thus we got into feeding animal protein to herbivores, which they said was disgusting. However, nobody came up with any arguments about consumers demanding cheap food.

I then gave out the 2 business cards for the farms (MYSTERIES RESOURCE SHEET 7) and asked which one was most likely to produce the healthiest food—eliciting the obvious response. I asked half the class to imagine that they were standing in the middle of Broadacre Farm and the other half in the middle of Loxley Coppice Farm. These students had done ***Mind Movies*** before (see page 39). I asked them collectively to spend a couple of minutes imagining what these farms would look like and then to write down their ideas. They got on with this so well that I gave up the idea of looking at the photographs, as it seemed superfluous. When I asked for the respective landscapes, they were able to give a fair run down on a very intensive arable farm—highly mechanised and 'modern' looking. The description of the organic farm was a bit too chocolate box for my liking, but they had mentioned woods, hedges, animals in fields, manure and stone buildings.

I showed the photograph of the free-range pigs (MYSTERIES RESOURCE SHEET 7).

Mysteries Exemplar 3: The lost livestock of Loxley Coppice Farm

Instructions

I organised three groups and gave out the envelopes, but told them not to open them (see MYSTERIES RESOURCE SHEET 8). They had done a ***Mystery*** before, so I gave them the central question: *'In recent months, piglets and chickens have been disappearing from Loxley Coppice Farm—you have to decide why this has been happening.'* I stressed that they should consider each piece of information carefully: it may or may not be relevant, but each should be considered. I reminded them that they were most likely to produce a good explanation by connecting pieces of information and ideas.

I told them to read carefully the information on the slips first and be prepared to ask if there were things that they did not understand. As there were only 9 students it did not seem necessary to have a formal slot for allowing them to seek clarification.

Managing the activity

It is worth emphasising here that management in such circumstances is little to do with behaviour and much to do with facilitating. I had to answer lots of questions, which initially were mainly factual, ie, *'Is free-range when the animals just wander around?'*, *'Are organic vegetables more expensive?'*, *'What is fallow?'*, and a variety of questions about support prices and CAP. As students' thoughts developed, the questions became much more speculative: *'So do you get more birds on organic farms?'* and *'Do organic farmers like wildlife like foxes?'* This presented me with a dilemma; I was really happy to answer the factual questions, especially if they related to syllabus relevant terms such as CAP, but I was reluctant to answer their later questions because I wanted them to use the evidence and think for themselves (not refer to me). So I started to say, *'Well, that is for you to work out'*. Some individuals were frustrated by this.

Students asking questions is a sign of thinking and therefore a good marker.

I was pleased that with very little prompting they were using knowledge both from other subjects and from their everyday lives. So, for example, two students who do biology talked about food webs and one of the girls who is very keen on riding knew enough about fox hunting to act as a source for the whole group. I could not resist, on a few occasions, shoving back the odd slip of paper under their noses and saying *'Are you sure that this has got nothing to do with it?'* It was an excellent lesson from my point of view. I do not know another way of getting a class to understand information better. The discussion, both in groups and whole class really helps them to clarify things. This strikes me as much more effective than the teacher talking.

This is yet another demonstration of the value of talking oneself 'into meaning'.

Follow-up

Although much understanding had been generated in this exercise there was a necessity to consolidate the outcomes. The problem was that the ***Mystery*** had touched on so many concepts and issues (partly addressed by sharing out the work).

1. One group drew farm system diagrams for the 2 farms, identifying the inputs, processes and outputs. I encouraged them to speculate where they did not have specific information.

Mysteries

Exemplar 3:

The lost livestock of Loxley Coppice Farm

2. One group drew a concept map (see article by Leat and Chandler in *Teaching Geography*, July 1996). The concepts could be distilled out by the students, but in this instance I delivered them: Government policies; landscape and environment; technology; market forces; animal welfare and morality. In short, the concept map encouraged students to determine the relationship between concepts which underlie an issue.

3. One group drew food webs for the two farms, using both the data and reasonable inference. They had a hard job with Broadacre Farm.

Each group had to do a 5-minute summary of their work and everybody got a copy of the concept maps, food webs and system diagrams. However, I know that at least two students redrew them to incorporate their own understanding. Finally, each student had to do an individual write-up of the initial question.

Farm Business Cards

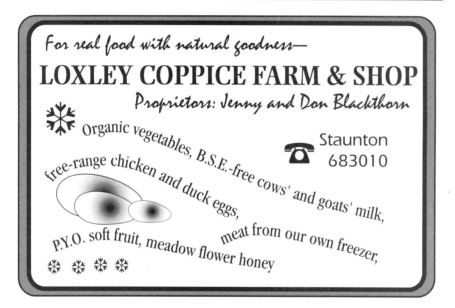

Mysteries Exemplar 3: The lost livestock of Loxley Coppice Farm

Free-range pigs

Mysteries Exemplar 3:

The lost livestock of Loxley Coppice Farm

Statements

1. Foxes are carnivores. They live in underground dens which are often enlarged rabbit burrows.

2. In Great Britain, between 1984 and 1990, 138,000km of hedges were removed; 75,000km of fences were constructed.

3. Rabbit burrows have appeared on the fairways and in the bunkers. The golf club has just called in a pest control company to deal with it.

4. Stoats and weasels eat eggs and chicks of groundnesting birds. Mice are vegetarian.

5. The Blackthorns use only natural fertilisers, such as manure, to keep their soil fertile.

6. The Blackthorns have just ordered higher fencing for their chicken run

7. Before sowing last year's crops Mr Massey amalgamated his fields; where there were 21 fields before there are now only 9.

8. Young Ryan Blackthorn has a diploma in hedge-laying from agricultural college.

9. Broadacres is an intensive arable farm using large quantities of pesticides, herbicides, chemical fertilisers and much machinery.

10. Mr Massey has recently bought a new crop sprayer and a very large combine harvester. The combine is more efficient in large fields.

11. To stop over-production of cereals, farmers receive grants from the EU to 'set aside' 20% of their arable land for other uses, such as fallow.

12. Mr Massey leases 20% of his farmland to a golf club. An old barn has been converted into a club house.

13. Government grants are available for: planting mixed woodland; creating wetland habitats; leaving arable land fallow.

14. Autumn-sown crops have become much more popular in recent years because they can be harvested earlier.

15. The Common Agricultural Policy (CAP) has, in the past, led to highly intensive farming, overproduction, and damage to the environment.

Continued...

Mysteries Exemplar 3: The lost livestock of Loxley Coppice Farm

16. The roots of trees and bushes help support rabbit burrows.

17. The co-operative that the Blackthorns belong to has just signed a contract with the Asbury supermarket chain to supply organic vegetables at top prices.

18. Cereal crops, hedges and long grass provide food and cover for birds and insects; around 20 species of mammal and 30 species of bird live in hedgerows.

19. Leythorpe Hunt is considering breeding foxes in captivity.

20. The Blackthorns have banned the Leythorpe hunt from crossing their land, despite strong local pressure.

21. All livestock on Loxley Coppice Farm is free-range.

22. Golfers complain about the smell from Loxley Coppice Farm especially when muckspreading.

23. Ray Massey is a qualified farm mechanic. He is also a good shot.

24. Loxley Coppice Farm has a large duck pond and newly-planted mixed woodland.

25. Over the last 25 years, some common farmland bird populations have been in steep decline: partridge 82%; song thrush 73%; skylark 58%; swallow 43%.

26. Many farmers have been losing livestock and rustling is suspected. An old van has been seen parked in odd places in country lanes.

27. There is a rapidly growing public interest in farm animal welfare and some demand for organically produced food.

28. If crops or weeds in 'set aside' are cut before late July many eggs and young birds are destroyed.

29. Cheap meat is often 'on offer' around local pubs.

30. The CAP-guaranteed prices encouraged farmers to grow as much food as possible, with grants for increasing the amount of land under production. This led to food mountains.

Statements Continued...

Mysteries: Adapting the strategy

Mysteries are very powerful and versatile and therefore can be devised for a whole range of subjects and topics:

- accidents and disasters;
- issues;
- decision making contexts;
- change contexts, whether associated with growth or decline.

They can be devised for human, economic and regional geography, but also physical geography where there is any human dimension at all. They do not require a huge amount of factual information, but a good understanding of the issues is required for planning. The ***Thinking Through Geography*** group have done them for:

- migration in both developed and developing economies;
- North Sea fishing;
- urban traffic problems;
- earthquakes;
- decline of rural services in Britain.

All these issues have strong cause and effect dimensions.

The following points should help.

- It is essential to have people in the data to personalise the events and to provide a narrative thread. The people make the Mystery accessible to low achieving students and interesting to everyone else. The mystery is a fragmented story, with intrigue and people to identify with and argue about. The narrative, or what happened/happens to the people are the trigger factors.
- There needs to be a central question to provide the motivation to start working with the statements. There can be further questions to extend the use of the data and context.
- The number of statements should be between 16 and 30. Below 16 there may not be enough ambiguity or data, and above 30 gets too complex and physically difficult to manage.
- There should be place, circumstance and time context, which tend to be the background factors. There may need to be reference to other places and earlier times.
- There could/should be some ambiguous, misleading or irrelevant statements. For example, one piece of information may be negated by another (just as clues and suspects get ruled out in police enquiries). However, be prepared for students creating a different interpretation and legitimately working into their explanation statements that were designed as red herrings.
- Additional resources such as maps and photos may be helpful to put some flesh on the bones.
- Textbooks, CD ROMs, videos, radio programmes, official reports and newspaper cuttings can all provide the starting point for creating a mystery. In reality you do not need a huge amount of factual information.

Afterthoughts

An example of scaffolding.

In our experience, the vast majority of students engage well and are motivated by ***Mysteries***, but inevitably there are some who lack the ability to work collaboratively and this is sometimes related to the individual's belief that the tasks are beyond them. Confidence grows if they can be helped to find some of the simpler relationships and only work with the data that they understand (see the industrial location example). It is striking that by the time a class does a second *Mystery* they are much better at it and have more confidence.

Mysteries represent the whole point about **teaching thinking approaches**. Students find them difficult at first, but it is because they find them difficult that we need to persevere with such approaches, because they require skills that are so important to becoming good learners. We cheat students in the end if we only ever give them things that they can readily do—they need to be challenged and extended to become better learners.

> *The curriculum needs to change the learner; ultimately, it is not justifiable always to water the curriculum down so that learners can cope—they need challenge.*

Story-telling

Rationale

Stories are powerful media. Stories are one of the ways in which societies transmit their culture from generation to generation. One of the few images we have of children being riveted at school is the infant class sitting on the floor while their teacher reads a story. And stories do not lose their fascination; the novel is narrative. Somehow teaching in secondary schools, perhaps with the exception of English, has lost its grip on story-telling. Telling stories in geography is not frivolous, or a distraction: it is a superb vehicle for teaching, especially when done with thought and care.

The advantages of **Story-telling** may be summarised as follows:

- stories put geography into real life contexts with real people (occasionally made up), providing topicality and relevance;
- stories provide a focus for developing listening skills, often sadly lacking in many students;
- stories are a vehicle for teaching students how to remember, which receives little explicit attention in the curriculum;
- story-boarding helps to develop sequencing skills which are essential in much explaining;
- using stories exposes students to extended pieces of text, rarely encountered elsewhere in geography, which therefore helps to prepare them for examination papers (at A Level) where such pieces of text are used;
- finally, as with the other strategies, **Story-telling** can be the key to unlocking understanding of one of geography's big concepts—causation.

This is a strong pedigree.

> *Being able to take in information efficiently is an important purpose of IE (Instrumental Enrichment).*

> *Story-telling helps the appeal to all the senses (see page 162).*

Story-telling Exemplar 1: Kingsley Osufu

Context

This activity was used with a middle band Y9 class and with a mixed ability Y10 group. Most of the detail given here relates to the Y10 group. The Y10 group were, with one or two exceptions, a pleasure to teach. The ability range was weighted more towards the bottom end, but what students lacked in ability, they made up for in motivation. The work was undertaken as part of a module on population and migration; they already had some understanding of push and pull factors and different types of migration.

The intended learning outcomes were mostly generic to the whole of GCSE, and therefore very important. Although migration provided a context and therefore some reinforcement to earlier lessons, I wanted to start students thinking about some vital skills for their GCSEs:

- to provide a number of models for remembering information;
- to develop an awareness of the importance and universal nature of cause and effect;
- to practise the planning of writing explanations.

In my view this was a highly successful lesson which had a long lasting pay off.

Preparation

The story was taken from broadsheet newspapers, so it was rewritten to reduce any problems created by language. This also allowed me to get to know the story really well and to create emphases that I wanted to convey. Stories with human drama make a tremendous difference to what students will comprehend. If they are hooked, they will make a real effort. Stories provide a tremendous context for learning and understanding new vocabulary. I rehearsed the story a few times so that I was familiar with it and could keep the flow going.

Subsequently I found some pictures of a motor engineering area in Kumasi in *Teaching Geography* ('Lessons from West Africa' by Tim Thomas & Jeff Serf, *Teaching Geography*, July 1994). I could show the sort of area that Kingsley might have been familiar with and which might have fuelled his ambitions.

I decided to work with groups of 3, so I made up appropriate trios, bearing in mind ability. I particularly wanted to have someone sensible and motivated to be the first person in each group. So I worked out the groups and allocated each student to be number 1, 2 or 3. It was a group of 25, so I had one reserve.

The strategy required sending 2 students from each group out of the room, for the first few minutes—two-thirds of the class! The most straightforward solution to this was to arrange with the librarian that I would send them there. However I have used a number of other solutions since.

Thinking Through Geography activities are not for the faint-hearted or the lazy—these hard aspects help make the difference.

Launching

This was an amenable class so I did not need to pull out all the stops. I started by saying *'Who remembers the story of Little Red Riding Hood?'* Most hands went up, there were some 'Yeahs'. I told them we often remember a story better than just a load of facts, because there is a thread to it: we can remember the sequence of events in a story because they are linked. *'Now imagine that you are sitting in a GCSE geography exam and you are trying to remember something about the causes of migration—but it just will not come and you are wasting time and getting worried. I am going to tell you a story that will help you, it is not just a doss and I am going to help you to remember stories better—so pay attention.'* It worked better than I had expected.

The word metacognition could be used here with the pupils so that they develop a vocabulary about learning.

Without more ado I read out the groups, numbering group members 1, 2 or 3 (a few grumbles were ignored). Two were away, so I used my reserve and I was short of a number 3. I told all the 2s and 3s (15 students) to go down to the library where they were expected and where they should sit quietly for a few minutes until called (on reflection I could have given them something to do).

Instructions

1. I told the number 1s to come to the front. I was going to read them a story which they had to try to remember, because they would be retelling it to the number 2s, who would retell it to the number 3s. They were not allowed to take notes (STORY-TELLING RESOURCE SHEET 1).

2. I read the story and at the end asked if there were any questions. There were a couple, one of which was about the name of the boat.

3. I sent one student to get the number 2s and told the rest to rehearse the story for retelling, allowing them to use paper now.

4. The number 2s arrived. I told them to sit with their number 1 who would tell them the story as they recalled it. The number 2s would be retelling it to the number 3s. The number 2s would be allowed to ask for clarification at the end of the story.

5. When the number 3s arrived I told them what I had told the number 2s. I also told the number 1s to listen carefully to the number 2s to see if they deviated or forgot things. I reminded them that the aim was to pass on the story as accurately as possible.

6. To finish, the number 3s had to retell the story to the number 1s with the number 2s listening.

Managing the activity

I imagine that some people will read this and say *'You must be joking'*. It is one of the riskier strategies, but I have only ever had to abandon it once. The two keys seem to be sense of purpose (this is important), and speed. You need everything to be fairly slick, with not much hanging around. For example, when you see that a few have finished **Story-telling** give a one minute warning.

When the number 1s are telling the story to the number 2s try to listen as carefully as possible to a couple. In my experience any silliness is most likely to occur with the number 2s retelling to the number 3s. Wisecrackers sometimes start to invent totally spurious passages, so monitor this carefully and crack down hard.

Debriefing

The more I do this activity the more important I realise it is because there are so many important cognitive skills used. Therefore my general advice is that the debriefing of a first attempt should be aimed at getting the students to see that learning how to remember is really worth working at. Do not be dismayed if this is an uphill struggle.

I started with an easy question: *'What did you remember?'* This produced a flurry of responses and I think gave the students some encouragement—at least I said *'Good, so we have proved that you do have brains'*. They laughed and joked dutifully.

Now I tried a harder question: *'How did you remember what you remembered?'* Silence. I am sure that they had never been asked this question in their lives.

I just waited and tried to look encouraging.

Eventually someone said: *'I pictured some of it. Like I could see it in a movie'.* When I asked *'like what?'* he replied, *'Well—the wet footprints for one thing'.* Again I was careful to say *'Good, well done. Anyone else?'* I would not say that it opened the floodgates, but the discussion did gather some momentum and several other very valuable points emerged about deliberately trying to remember things:

Story-telling Exemplar 1: Kingsley Osufu

An important cognitive skill.

There is a high premium on sophisticated classroom skills here.

Story-telling Exemplar 1: Kingsley Osufu

All these points show some metacognitive awareness developing.

Constructivism at work (see page 157).

- don't try to remember too much unimportant detail like the name of the boat or what port it started from—it just 'clogs up the brain';
- try to remember the story as a sequence, a chain of events ('this led to this which led to this'), then you are more aware of having missed something when you try to remember it. One bit triggers off the rest;
- for a few students turning the story into a map in their heads was helpful and they could remember certain events by where they happened on the mental map—this tended to be the more able who could picture the coast of Africa;
- some students could picture and remember things much better if they had some personal experience of it—they could picture the main cargo hold and the deck (from movies?) but they could not picture the forward hold that the stowaways were moved to;
- two students said that they thought it helps to invent a moral or a point for the story like 'crime never pays' (in relation to the sailors);
- some points are just very memorable, like the dockworker's card hidden in the sacks to prove to the police that Kingsley had been on the boat.

This illustrates the continuing need for further debriefing skills.

I don't think that I was successful in consolidating all these points as I did not know what they would say until they said it, but I found it fascinating. You are always better prepared a second time around. We did end on the general point that **remembering is a skill that can be learned** and that we could apply it to everyday problems as well as learning for exams.

Follow-up

The follow-up is a very significant feature of this strategy. I regard the activity above as a way to get their brains moving. It is like all the effort to move a big boulder. Once you have got them thinking, it is important to make something of the momentum before it stops again.

To this end I used story-boarding in the next lesson. Students were given the base story-board boxes (STORY-TELLING RESOURCE SHEET 2), with 8 story frames and 4 cause and 4 effect frames, and were asked to retell the story using just the 8 story frames. As they work in A4 size exercise books these could be stuck onto a double-page spread. They were shown how these could be laid out with an OHP.

A similar approach may benefit some of the other strategies.

It is strongly recommended that you think carefully about whether you want them to use the story-board sheets as they are, get the pupils to draw out their own frames, or cut out and paste the frames into their files/books. The latter two options allow greater flexibility. You need to give clear instructions.

Further they were only allowed to use 8 words for each frame (you can go to 10 or 12, but using more defeats the purpose of brevity and clarity). This encourages students to be very selective in their choice of words and the selection of the important events in the story. They were asked to do it in pencil, so that they could amend it, but of course a few did not have pencils. I was amazed at how difficult they found this, which reinforced the thought that we were doing something important.

Two common problems occurred. Firstly, using up 3 frames early in the story-board when 1 would do (which I put down to bad planning). Secondly, difficulty in summarising in a few words, so I had to relent slightly on the 8-word limit. I have realised now, after using story-boards several times with the same class, that they really need to plan before they write by asking questions such as, *'What are the really important points?'* and *'What roughly is the mid-way point that should be in frame 4 and what is the end point that should be in frame 8?'* Over 3 or 4 attempts I have noted a substantial improvement in their ability to write in the 8 frames. When I asked them to do a case study story-board as part of a GCSE

There are more pointers to metacognition about the writing process.

Story-telling Exemplar 1: Kingsley Osufu

question, I explained that this was in order to practise putting a lot of information into a small space without losing the end or conclusion. They seemed to accept this point, although I could not say whether this has improved their exam writing technique. Some students have said that they like doing the frames because it helps them organise their thoughts, but equally one or two have said *'boring'* when I mention story-boards. You cannot please all the people all of the time!

Debriefing on the story-boarding part focused on how you decide what to write and what events to include. One of the best suggestions was to imagine the story as 8 stills (as in a cartoon or comic) and then use the words to explain what is happening. Another common comment was *'cut out the adjectives'* (which I must admit has caused me to worry whether they would cut out adjectives in their exam writing). It is worth asking one or two students to read out their story for public comment on how it could be improved. I try to choose fairly good ones to avoid embarrassment and to share some of the better thinking, but the real benefit here is that they have come to accept that drafting and thinking about their writing in order to improve it, is worth doing. I have subsequently come across a whole project about writing frames (Lewis & Wray, 1995) and I feel that the use of story-boards fulfils exactly the same function.

Finally you can also use cause and effect frames. You will see on the story-board (STORY-TELLING RESOURCE SHEET 2) that there are 4 boxes marked respectively cause and effect. Students are asked to write in the frames (again 8-12 words) to give the cause of Kingsley's decision to stowaway to France and to speculate in the effects frames on the consequences of the events. Students are given freedom as to how exactly they use the frames. They can give 4 different causes, use 2 frames on each of 2 causes or use all 4 frames for a major cause or effect. I find that it helps to get the students to focus on geographical issues, although I am slightly fearful that they leave things out that they think are not geographical but that I would like to see in, such as the effects on Kingsley's family. This works a treat because they can see visually that causes precede events and effects follow on. I have even encouraged some to do thumbnail sketches in the boxes to aid visualisation. I am forming the view that it is better to get students to do at least 2 causes because exam questions rarely ask for only one reason or cause. I think that these story-boards will be a real asset in revising for C, D and E candidates.

Two big concepts are being developed here. If students did these exemplars and several Mysteries, they would have an unusual and valuable grasp of the concepts of cause and effect (see pages 167–168).

As a further task, with more able groups who are restricted by the story-board, a longer piece of written work can be done.

Story-telling Exemplar 1: Kingsley Osufu

Kingsley's story—based on an article by Julian Nundy from The Guardian, 11 December 1995

Kingsley Osufu, aged 24, was a casual dockworker at Takoradi, one of the ports in Ghana. Often Kingsley went home to his wife Agnes with nothing after a day spent waiting for work that never came. He won some money in the lottery and saw his chance. In October 1992, Kingsley (along with seven others, one of them his brother, Albert) stowed away aboard the Ukrainian ship *MC Ruby* which was carrying a cargo of timber and cocoa to Europe. Kingsley left his wife who was expecting their first child in Ghana. He wished to go to Europe to receive training so that he could return to Ghana as an engineer.

The eight of them hid in a hold full of expectation. However, they eventually ran out of supplies and two of them went to look for water after a day or so when they had plucked up the courage to leave their safe hideaway. The two people who went to find water found four other stowaways who had got on board at Cameroon. They also were trying to go to Europe. They shared out the food that they had brought and exchanged stories of what they would do when they got to Europe. However, they did not realise that when they had gone to get the water they had left footprints on the deck.

The next morning six sailors appeared armed with knives and revolvers. 'Who are you? Where are you from?' they asked in English. Kingsley quickly became the group's spokesperson and told the sailors where they had embarked. The sailors then asked if they had money and Kingsley replied that they did. 'Get it ready and we will come back to put you up somewhere else', one said.

That evening the sailors returned and, taking the money led the stowaways to the bow of the ship where they pushed them through a hatch into a space like a storage tank. One morning a sailor opened the hatch to throw down three bottles of water. Otherwise they were given nothing and were left to live in their own filth for three days.

In the early hours of 3rd November, after ten days at sea, the hatch opened and two sailors ordered the men out 'in groups of two or three'. Finally only Kingsley and Albert

Continued...

Story-telling Exemplar 1: Kingsley Osufu

remained. When the two sailors came for them they noticed the other four standing in the shadows. Some had blood on their clothes.

Kingsley asked where the other stowaways had gone. A sailor responded by hitting him across the head with an iron bar. He broke free and ran along the deck; he turned in time to see two men throw Albert into the sea. Some of the sailors opened fire on him but missed. He managed to reach number three hold and hid amongst sacks of cocoa.

For the next three days he hid while every morning and evening the sailors searched the hold.

One evening, the *MC Ruby* docked. As the engines stopped Kingsley left his hideaway. Filling his pocket with cocoa beans and hiding his Ghanaian dockers work-card under a sack, he climbed up a ventilation shaft and forced open the rusty grill at its mouth.

Early on the morning of 6th November he jumped to the quay side and ran towards a street-cleaning vehicle. The two operators spoke no English but pointed him in the direction of the harbour police. He eventually found the police station. At 4am he began his story. Looking at the wall he saw a map, on it was the word France. Until then he had not known where he was.

After daybreak the Le Havre police searched the *MC Ruby*. They found Mr Osufu's work-card. Still terrified he was allowed to watch an identity parade on the deck hidden behind a porthole to identify his six tormentors.

The investigators concluded that five members of the crew and Captain Vladimir Ilnitsky were responsible. They were charged with offences ranging from complicity to murder to extortion, kidnapping and acts of piracy. Four admitted the crime immediately, two denied it, those who admitted their role said they were worried because of the heavy fines imposed on the shipping companies whose vessels bring stowaways into European ports.

Story-board

**Story-telling
Exemplar 1: Kingsley Osufu**

Cause			Effect
Cause			Effect
Cause			Effect
Cause			Effect

Story-telling Exemplar 2: The Lynmouth floods

Context

This exemplar was done with a Y12 A Level group studying floods and flood management, a topic common to nearly all syllabuses. We had in the previous weeks spent some considerable time working on hydrographs (see follow-up). There were 18 in the group with a broad spread of most student characteristics.

I did not think that the use of *Story-telling* was as crucial to this group as to the *Kingsley Osufu* group, but I am gradually refining my ideas about this. I used this format to extend the variety of teaching techniques to maintain interest. A Level can be heavy going at times and it is important to maintain enthusiasm.

Preparation

The Lynmouth flood story has always been one of my favourite resources. The fact that it has stayed with me demonstrates the power of a good story. Stories about people going through dramatic events (with a liberal dose of death and destruction) get you hooked (I hope that does not sound too callous).

It is a long text and difficult to condense without losing some of its power, so I used it as it was. I could not send students off to other parts of the school because they would be away too long. I re-read it a couple of times to remind myself of the detail and pattern.

If you have less than 12 in the group you may need to rethink the instructions given below.

Launching

If it is the first time that you have used *Story-telling* with the group, you could use a similar approach to Exemplar 1. I have recently made up a new story to accompany this activity (I believe in a few fibs for a good cause)— *'You may not know this but I have an Auntie Lyn. She is my mother's sister* (or my sister if you are much older than me). *She was born on August 15th, 1952. I am going to tell you a story that not only explains why she was called Lyn, but also why she spells her name differently from most Lynns, that is with only one N.'*

Instructions

1. Divide the class into groups of 6 and give them a number 1-6 within each group.
2. Tell them that each number needs to listen out for what happens to a particular character or characters:
   (1) John Pedder;
   (2) Charles Postles;
   (3) Tom Bevan;
   (4) John and Cleeva Loosemore;
   (5) the Jenkins family;
   (6) Derek Harper.

As the characters crop up students need to make notes on what happened to them, but they should not worry if they miss some.

3. Each person needs to listen out for one other thing and make notes. This means that generally everybody has to listen all the way through:
   (6) What Lynmouth, the valley and the area were like?
   (5) What were the causes of the flood?
   (4) Who, where and how people died?
   (3) What buildings were damaged? How were they damaged?
   (2) What other damage and destruction occurred?
   (1) What was done to rescue people, clear up the mess and repair the damage?

The names and questions act as advance organisers for listening—see also 'Down and Out in Sunderland' (Mind Movies, Exemplar 3—see pages 45–50).

Story-telling Exemplar 2: The Lynmouth floods

This is an example of working as groups, rather than just in groups (see pages 160).

4. Read the story with suitable dramatic effect and some slight pauses to allow for the scribbling of notes, but don't get too slow.
5. Put all the 1s together, all the 2s together, etc, and ask them to pool their notes—allow only 5 minutes.
6. Put them back into the original groups and ask them to go round in turn and give their 2 summaries. Encourage them to make notes from the sharing, but again to a tight time limit.
7. Now give them the story-board and get them to reduce the events, excluding the causes and effects to 10 frames. Emphasise that they cannot include all the characters: they can only include them as examples; or even leave them out. They should be trying to show the general sequence and general pattern: what sort of thing happened first; what happened next; what happened at the end. Also emphasise that the frames should follow on logically from one another (this was much more obvious with the Kingsley Osufu story—see Exemplar 1).
8. Finally, the cause and effect frames had to be added. Remember that this class had experienced story-boarding before.

Managing the activity

The management requirements are slightly different here compared to the first exemplar: generally it was easier. However, it was important to monitor the work of the groups of 1s, 2s, 3s, etc, and later the groups of 1-6. In the case of the former, I nominated someone in each group to start telling the rest of the group what they had noted down. I tried to choose someone fairly outgoing, but not necessarily the most able, because I wanted the group to be able to improve their notes collectively, rather than just copy down the efforts of the best. This is not always possible, but I keep working on them to share, question and clarify and not just copy.

In the case of the 1-6 groups it is impossible for them to work as one large group as some get left out and some opt out. So once they have shared their information I split them into pairs to work on the story-boards (see Exemplar 1, but note that they were allowed more cause and effect boxes here). It is important also to set time limits.

Thinking Through Geography activities are generally powerful diagnostic assessment tools because they hinge on crucial skills.

Students found the story-boarding much harder than I had expected, I think because of the complication added by all that happened to the characters in the story. The end products were very variable; 3 of the students found it almost impossible to sort out a logical sequence. Ironically I think that this highlights the important diagnostic value of the activity, because these students (and others) also find it hard to write reasoned sequential arguments in essays. Of the more able students, most enjoyed the process, but one complained that it would have been much easier to take notes.

Debriefing

Time was short, so I did not debrief as much as I might, and (if I am honest) I ended up telling them more than I might have wished. So, through a combination of questioning and telling, I established the following:

- most of what had happened to the characters was included in the 10 boxes, whereas the information from the six questions had ended up in the cause and effect boxes;
- the background factors or causes were furthest to the left, ie, at the beginning of the chain of explanation; the trigger factors, such as the electricity going off, were further along the chain (the exception to this was the heavy rain);

- the effects could be seen as short or long term: this comes out visually in the story-board format, the long term being furthest to the right;
- sequencing was really important in developing explanation and argument; in a sequence one point must lead to another and be related to it.

Follow-up

The instructions, given above, contain the immediate follow-up. However, one further activity was added in a following lesson when the students were asked to draw a simple hydrograph underneath their story-board, thus uniting the sequence of events with the storm events. This was a neat way of demonstrating the interaction of physical and human systems.

Story-telling Exemplar 2: The Lynmouth floods

More elaboration of cause and effect.

Story-telling Exemplar 2: The Lynmouth floods

Lynmouth's ordeal by flood

Source: Geography 14–18: Water and Rivers

The deluge engulfed one of Devon's loveliest villages, bringing terror and havoc.

IT HAD rained steadily since mid-morning. By 3 p.m. that Friday, August 15, 1952, the sky was so overcast that street and house lights went on in Lynmouth. But still the tourists' cars crawled cautiously down Lynmouth Hill, a narrow, steep road with a gradient in parts of one in four, to pack the quayside of the picturesque fishing village.

Every cafe in Lynmouth was crowded with visitors. They lingered over their Devon cream teas, listening to the rain drumming down and watching the water surging through the harbour. Lynmouth stands at the end of a narrow, wooded valley, where the East and West Lyn rivers finish their 500 metre descent from Exmoor and merge to flow into the Bristol Channel. Postcards show the combined stream as clear and shallow, rippling over a rocky bed: now it was a murky torrent, rising fast.

No one had reason to suspect Lynmouth was about to be overwhelmed by disaster. As a local explained: 'The river often comes up even higher. It soon goes down again.'

But some began to wonder. In the East Lyn valley, 17-year-old John Pedder, son of the Lynmouth postmaster, was fishing the foaming river for trout when he noticed an uncanny feeling in the air. At 6.30 p.m. it was almost as dark as night. He had never seen such rain. With a sense of foreboding he started out for home.

And engineer Charles Postles, in his house behind Lynmouth power station, Was enjoying high tea at the end of a day's duty when a bell rang to recall him to the station. Water was leaking through the roof on to one of the alternators. He rigged a tarpaulin to cover it, then stayed to keep an eye on the river running beside the station. It had to rise only three metres more to overflow its banks, and even as he watched it was climbing towards the danger mark. To his astonishment, he saw trees drifting past. Then there was a rumbling sound, and Postles told an assistant: 'We're in for trouble. Those are boulders moving along the river bed.'

To Tom Bevan, the Lynmouth-born proprietor of the Lyndale Hotel, in the heart of the village, there still seemed no serious danger. He noticed that the East Lyn had changed colour from muddy brown to black, and smelt of peat, hut the water hadn't yet reached the flight of steps from the road to his ground floor.

Nor was Mrs. Cleeva Loosemore at the riverside Nelson Tea Rooms unduly worried as she prepared a roast duck birthday dinner for her husband, John, who was on Exmoor, driving one of their staff home. When he telephoned to ask what it was like in Lynmouth, she told him: 'Spray is splashing against the kitchen windows—hut I've lived here too long to be scared of the river.'

By now, boats in the harbour were snapping their moorings and drifting out to sea. In the power station, Charles Postles watched the river rise and spread across the floor of the building. When the spinning flywheels of the generators picked up water and flung it on the switchboard, he had no choice but to black out the village.

It was 7.30. In the gloom of his candle-lit hotel, Tom Bevan was becoming anxious about his young daughters, who had gone to a concert party at the Pavilion on the seafront, near the harbour. When he left the hotel to fetch them the road was flooded knee-deep, so he took a hillside path through the woods. Inside the darkened theatre, he found a comedian leading the audience in community singing to keep up their spirits.

Continued...

> **Story-telling Exemplar 2: The Lynmouth floods**

First Fatality. Most of the audience, including Bevan's daughters, followed him back along the path, but a few chose to make their own way to their hotels. Seven holidaymakers were seen to link arms and set off along the seafront towards the harbour. As they turned a corner, they met the swollen river racing down the street. The chain broke—and the woman at the end was swept out to sea.

The rush to escape was on. John Pedder went to help his father save what they could from the Post Office, one of the shops on the narrow main street which bordered the river. They were hurriedly filling some wire baskets when a tree trunk cannoned through the wall. The river poured in after it, and the heavy wooden counter became wedged in a corner. They retreated to a back room, escaping through the skylight, and into the next-door house, with £1,300 worth of stock.

All along the street, firemen and volunteers were evacuating villagers by rope and ladder. In one cottage, children were trapped in a groundfloor room. A group of men formed a human chain across the swirling water, broke the cottage windows, and caught the youngsters as they floated out.

Up on Exmoor, John Loosemore had desperately been trying to get back to Lynmouth. But whichever way he turned, bridges were down and roads inundated. The day's rainfall was fast approaching a near-record twenty-three centimetres—equivalent to more than 22,500 million litres dumped on the ninety square kilometres of thin peat crust covering impervious rock.

Loosemore forced his car on to the only patch of high ground within reach, and in the flickering lightning looked out on an astonishing spectacle. 'The whole of Exmoor,' he said later, 'seemed one mass of water.'

All across the northern slopes of the moor, a network of 14 bursting tributaries cascaded into the East and West Lyn rivers—each falling to the sea in narrow gorges, ripping twenty-seven metre trees from the banks and rolling ten-tonne boulders towards Lynmouth like so many skittles.

Just before the two rivers met in the centre of Lynmouth to run into the harbour, they passed under separate bridges. At Lyndale Bridge, beside the Lyndale Hotel, the seventeen metre arch was broad enough for debris coming down the East Lyn to tumble through. The West Lyn bridge, though, was only nine metres wide. First it became jammed with trees: then thousands of boulders piled up. Behind this barrier the river rose, burst its bank and changed course, joining the East Lyn upstream of Lyndale Bridge.

On the groundfloor of the Lyndale Hotel, built seven metres above street level, guests had been crowding at the windows, watching the East Lyn race past below and congratulating themselves on being, as Tom Bevan said, in 'the safest possible place.' But at 9.30 the swing doors at the side burst open. A wall of water smashed through. Fifty people ran for their lives to the first floor; then, as the river crept up the stairs, they climbed to the second floor. Bevan hurried to the family wing to collect his wife's jewellery, and as he opened the door, saw the far wall disintegrate. Just in time he reached the stairs.

The raging river now carried all before it: furniture from gutted houses, cars, even a 36-seater bus. It ripped away the corners of two more hotels and completely destroyed another which had already been evacuated—then went on to wreck the stone Baptist chapel, the lifeboat house, the old Rhenish Tower lighthouse, on the quay. A torch was seen to light up in a cottage which promptly collapsed as though pressing the torch button had triggered a bomb. One moment there was a telephone kiosk with a woman inside it, making a call; the next, it had vanished.

Advancing Tide. By ten o'clock, as the rain continued, destruction was spreading back up the valleys. 800 metres from Lynmouth, three elderly people died when the East Lyn beat down Middleham Cottages. Meanwhile, on the Lynmouth-Barnstaple road the West Lyn was fast climbing towards Barbrook Cottages, a row of twelve

Continued...

Story-telling Exemplar 2: The Lynmouth floods

semi-detached council houses standing some seven metres above the river.

First to notice that the water had risen four metres in five minutes was Fred Jenkins, at No. 9. His wife, Ellen, went to fill a kettle and called out: 'The tap water's black.' As she put a tin bath outside the front door, hoping to collect some rainwater instead, the bath was snatched from her hands. The river was overflowing on to the road.

At the end house of the row, No. 12, Ellen Jenkins' nephews—the three Williams boys—were listening to the storm and waiting for their parents to come home. When the kitchen floor fell in, they climbed out of a window on to the road, now flooded waist deep. Their grandparents, Tom and Mary Floyd, were still inside No. 11: then, as though in slow motion, both No. 11 and No. 12 slid into the river.

Multiple Tragedy. While the boys were fighting to reach safety, Ellen and Fred Jenkins left No. 9, which was then on the point of toppling, and clung to the railings outside. They watched helplessly as their house was swept away, then, seconds later, as Mrs. Emily Ridd's house next door—No. 10—was claimed by the river. Inside were Mrs. Ridd, her grandson and two Australian girl hikers to whom she had given shelter just half an hour before.

As Ellen Jenkins stared into the darkness, she felt something brush against her. Instinctively, she caught hold. It was her father, Tom Floyd—half drowned and sole survivor of the nine people in No. 11. So loud was the rush of water, so black the night, that tenants of the remaining eight houses knew nothing of their neighbours' plight. When the Jenkinses sought refuge, the woman who opened the door to them said: 'You can't come in here in that state, you'll spoil my carpet.'

In the small hours of August 16, the storm passed its peak. Six Lynmouth firemen were as yet unable to help with rescue work; before the worst of the flooding began, they had gone with their tender to pump out waterlogged farmhouses at the top end of the valley. Police Constable Derek Harper went with them—and narrowly escaped death when the bridge at Barbrook collapsed under him. Returning, the party found themselves cut off. With all bridges down, it took hours of manhandling trees, rocks and fallen telephone poles off the only possible road before they managed to clear a path for the fire tender. When they reached shattered Lynmouth at three a.m., the rivers were at last receding.

Working through the night, Harper and the firemen rescued many people trapped in shops and houses, and took them to the Lyndale Hotel—clambering up the boulders and through a window, to join Tom Bevan and his beleaguered guests on the second floor. At first light all were evacuated, followed by other villagers and several hundred holidaymakers who climbed through the hotel, then crossed the river and reached the Tors Hotel on Countisbury Hill, from where they were taken to Minehead.

The scene of devastation that calm and sunny Saturday morning was appalling. As rescue workers converged on Lynmouth from all over

Continued...

Picture (a)

Story-telling Exemplar 2: The Lynmouth floods

Picture (b)

Devon and Somerset, they found the sea had turned brown and was littered with flotsam. The village itself, pounded by the rivers and 100,000 tonnes of boulders, looked as though it had been blitzed.

More than 90 houses and other buildings were destroyed or, like the battered Lyndale Hotel, would have to be demolished. Some 130 cars were wrecked, 19 boats lost. Drowned animals were scattered on the foreshore.

The storm had taken 34 lives—9 men, 16 women, 9 children. 22 villagers were killed, 11 holidaymakers and one unidentified woman.

It seemed impossible that the stricken village could ever recover. But as refugees found billets in Lynmouth and Minehead, the first of a fleet of bulldozers and excavators were already crossing Exmoor. The area was sealed off to the public for nearly three weeks, and one of the biggest combined emergency operations ever mounted in peacetime got under way—the Army, alone, contributing more than 1,000 men.

Welcome Help. When a relief fund was opened two days after the storm, the response from those who knew and loved Lynmouth was overwhelming. More than 12,000 gift parcels came from every corner of Britain, and citizens of 17 countries contributed such a torrent of money that 40,000 cheques arrived in a single day. In little more than two months, £1.25 million had been raised to help villagers who had lost homes and families.

Slowly a new Lynmouth began to take shape, with roads and bridges rebuilt and widened, river walls strengthened, the harbour restored. It took about two and a half years and cost £725,000 before the job was finished. But today, the village shows no outward sign of its ordeal. Though the summer visitor finds it difficult to visualize the horror of that August night many years ago, there are many people still living in Lynmouth who can never forget—like Tom Bevan, who had looked out of his hotel to see in the flaring lightning a maelstrom of tumbling rocks and trees and water. 'It seemed as though the whole valley was trying to engulf us. I can't believe it, even now.'

END

Picture (c)

Story-telling Exemplar 3: The Nevado del Ruiz volcanic eruption

Context

I used this activity as a final session for the KS3 tectonic processes module with a Y9 class. In the previous six weeks the pupils had covered the distribution of volcanoes followed by an in-depth study of earthquakes. Time was running out, and I considered omitting volcanoes altogether, but I felt that this would cheat my pupils somewhat! Therefore I needed one lesson that would:

- capture their imagination;
- make them think;
- help them to build on their understanding of hazards;
- give them images to remember.

Story-telling fitted the bill exactly—it was also near the end of term and I did not want to give in to the calls for *'games please'*. **Story-telling** provided an informal approach and a great deal of potential for learning.

Preparation

As in Exemplar 1, the vital part of the preparation is planning for having two-thirds of the class out of the room. In this case, we had some Initial Teacher Training students in the humanities faculty, so I could call on a colleague who was free to supervise them. I planned a short, straightforward activity for them to do during their time outside.

The room was arranged so that all the tables were pushed to the sides leaving a good space in the centre. The chairs were placed in a horseshoe facing me.

For this activity we have used two different resources with different classes. With this particular class the resource used was STORY-TELLING RESOURCE SHEET 4.

Launching

The pupils were 'high' when they arrived and seemed to expect a lazy lesson. As the room had been rearranged, they were thrown a bit and started to speculate about what would happen. As they came in they were told that they should put their bags on the tables and sit down—they did not need any equipment. Once they were seated, I explained that we had reached the end of the work on earthquakes and that we could only fit in one lesson on volcanoes. Therefore it had to be one that they would remember well, so I had decided to tell them a story. There was some consternation at this, especially from those who felt that they had outgrown this sort of nonsense! I explained that the process of active Story-telling really helps us to remember, and therefore they weren't just going to be passive listeners, but that they would be retelling it to each other. Gradually they were becoming interested.

Instructions

1. Pupils were numbered off 1-3, cutting across friendship groups.
2. The 2s and 3s left the room and the 1s sat together in the horseshoe.
3. I explained to the 1s that they would have to listen very carefully so that they could retell the story to the second group. The stages in this process are:
    (a) listen to the story;
    (b) discuss with each other what they could remember, and what they were unsure about;
    (c) agree on three questions that they wanted to ask me to clarify details of the story;

> (d) decide how the group should retell the story so that each of them contributed;
>
> (e) retell the story to the 2s once they entered and sat opposite them.
>
> 4. I read the story, pausing slightly a few times to help them visualise what was happening.

Story-telling Exemplar 3: The Nevado del Ruiz volcanic eruption

Managing the activity

For me, a crucial aspect of managing this activity was the arrangement of the room, which helped create a sense of purpose and allowed me to keep a track on things. The 1s worked well together, asked their three questions and needed no intervention from me. They decided that they would go in order and tell the 2s one thing each about the events.

This would be an excellent example of learning through collaborative talk.

The 2s then went though exactly the same process, except that they asked the 1s the clarifying questions, rather than me. The 2s used their questions to clarify the sequence of events, which was somewhat lost in the 1's story-telling. While the 2s told the story to the 3s, the 1s were out of the room. The 2s told the story in a rough order of events with each pupil choosing an aspect they could remember and claimed to understand. To me it seemed easier to follow, even though there were pauses and different interpretations.

The 3s asked their questions and planned their version and told this to the reassembled class (you could send the 2s out if you wished). The 1s now had to identify what was missing or inaccurate, as only they had heard the original. Amazingly the main threads of the story were there, and although there were some omissions, most of the last account was accurate.

Debriefing

For the debriefing, we stayed in the horseshoe arrangement. Initially I asked questions from the front either of individuals or of whole groups. Before too long the pupils were arguing and debating amongst themselves about the events. I endeavoured to make sure that it was a whole class discussion but with only one person speaking at a time.

I focused on the listening and remembering aspects to begin with:

What did you find easiest to remember and why?

- blood and gore and dismembered bodies;
- view from the plane;
- because it was easy to visualise;
- because it was an extreme or exciting situation.

What did you find most difficult to remember and why?

- Spanish and other unfamiliar names or words;
- numbers.

How did you try to remember?

- imagine being in a plane and the view from above;
- imagine being a survivor, thinking about what could be seen, smelt and heard;
- using analogies such as 'like a beach at low tide', which were easier to visualise as familiar images—volcanoes are unfamiliar and harder to visualise.

All these responses can contribute over time to metacognition about remembering.

Story-telling Exemplar 3: The Nevado del Ruiz volcanic eruption

I also asked:

'Did everyone remember the same things?'

'Do some people have a better ability for remembering things?'

'Can we all learn this skill?'

We then focused on the aspect of retelling the story. It was generally agreed that the 2s had been quite successful and, although the 1s had included all the information, the loss of story sequence made for poorer understanding. We did not spend much time taking the story apart as a case study of a volcanic eruption as we did not have the time or particularly the need. If it was a GCSE group this would have been much more important.

The final part of the debrief focused on what skills they had developed during this session. Responses included:

- listening;
- visualising;
- selecting important information;
- sequencing;
- discussing;
- choosing good questions;
- co-operating;
- communicating;
- explaining effectively;
- having confidence.

Pupils also picked up on the issue of third hand information. With this group I did not feel it was desperately important to emphasise too much the relevance of these skills in revision and examinations. Instead we concentrated on the personal and social skills and those skills that would help get more out of reading or listening to the teacher, each other or listening to videos.

The eruption of the Nevado del Ruiz, Colombia, 14 November 1985

Story-telling Exemplar 3: The Nevado del Ruiz volcanic eruption

Source: *The Challenge of the Natural Environment,* (Knapp, Ross, McCrae)

'Colombia Landslide worst since Krakatoa'

20,000 feared dead after volcano erupts

From Tony Jenkins in Bogotá

As many as 20,000 people may have died in western Colombia after a long-dormant volcano in the Andes erupted and sent torrents of mud and water flooding the town of Armero.

Dismembered bodies were washed downstream in flood waters stained with sulphur as rescuers struggled to reach the scene. Colombian civil defence units reported that seven villages had also been destroyed.

The busy riverside town of Armero, with a population of 28,000, was devastated before dawn while its inhabitants were sleeping. If early estimates are confirmed the death toll will be the highest from a volcanic eruption since the eruption in Martinique in 1902.

Nevado del Ruiz stands nearly 18,000 feet high in the northern Andes, and its eruption caused an icecap and snow on the peak to melt. Together with torrential rainfall, the water burst the banks of the river La Laguinilla. Two hours after the eruption the melting snow also sparked an avalanche.

The mud, rocks, and water flooded through Armero and swept away 85 per cent of the town. Captain Fernando Cervera, a Colombian airline pilot who flew over Armero yesterday, said: 'It's Dantesque. It looks like a beach at low tide, just mud and driftwood. Trees, houses, and cars were all carried off'.

The captain said that a few houses were still standing, and that the roofs were crowded with people waiting to be rescued.

Captain Cervera said that the volcano threw smoke 26,000 feet into the air, and filled the cabin of his plane with smoke.

Source: *The Times,* 14 November 1985

'I had to ask the passengers to use their oxygen masks,' he told Radio Caracol, after diverting his plane from a scheduled landing at Bogotá to Cali. He said that visibility was so bad 'we did not know it was an eruption.'

Local radio crews struggled for 12 hours to get through to Armero—which is only 150 miles from the capital Bogotá—because a half dozen bridges had been swept away and the road is covered in mud. After being there for only an hour they were obliged to withdraw, as the landslides continued to advance on what was left of the road.

Story-telling: Adapting the strategy

Three slightly different formats have been used in the three exemplars. In the first and last exemplars two-thirds of the class are sent from the class during the initial *Story-telling*. In the first case, the subsequent retelling is done by individual to individual and, in the last case, it is done from group to group. In the second exemplar all the pupils are kept in the room and they focus on different aspects of the story leading to a pooling of information.

All three variants can be used in other contexts. The biggest difficulty is in finding the stories. Newspapers are the most likely source, but it is worth keeping the need in mind as you read novels (if you get the time). One of our colleagues has also used songs, most notably *'Gold Rush Brides'* (by Ten Thousand Maniacs) which is about migration. It is fairly important that the story has a discernible time line through it, either in terms of times and dates or sequencing clues.

We strongly recommend the use of story-boarding as it greatly magnifies the possible benefits. We would also advise that this is potentially one of the best activities in the book for getting pupils to talk about how they have done a task and thus get them started on talking about learning. It can fall flat—but 'nothing ventured nothing gained!'

Afterthoughts

The Nevado del Ruiz lesson requires some further comment. It was an extremely satisfying lesson. Students were involved in an extended period of co-operation and I really felt that they appreciated the value of sharing information and ideas. There seemed to be a cross-fertilisation with the weaker pupils, or those who find concentration difficult, being drawn into the process and gaining as much as the stronger pupils. As such it differentiated well. Because no written work was required and full participation was expected it allowed all pupils to make valid contributions at their own level. It also gave me a good opportunity to observe peer group interactions and listen in on a debate being held within just one group at a time whilst the others were out of the room. The support teacher who works with the statemented pupils was very positive about the activity as she felt they had been listened to and treated as equals by their classmates.

Behaviour of disruptive pupils is often improved in Thinking Through Geography activities. See also the DTM Living Graph exemplar (see pages 24–27).

The final selling point for me came at the end of the lesson when one boy, usually characterised by disaffection and a special ability to distract others, stuck his hand up. We had been debriefing for about 20 minutes and he obviously wanted to prove to us (and I think to himself) that he could still remember all the details. He asked if he could retell the whole story to everyone before the bell went. Much encouraged by the others he did so, with a real flourish. A very satisfying end to the lesson.

More generally, if you have knowledge of or interest in learning styles, you may make the connection that this strategy may well appeal to pupils whose natural preferences in terms of learning may not be met in many other lessons.

This is an important point for those who indulge in this book at Level 4—developing a whole curriculum (see page 2).

One of the consequences of a 10-subject National Curriculum is that important generic skills are lost sight of. Everybody is too busy with content to worry about things which are not mentioned in PoS. So it is with **listening** as an active process. Admittedly, listening is a core skill in English, but it seems isolated in that one enclave of the curriculum. In our limited experience, teaching about listening pays dividends, because so much of human transaction is carried out through talk.

Fact or Opinion?

Rationale

Many current geographical issues are based around differing viewpoints (eg, the causes of acid rain and global warming). As geographers and teachers we have the task of presenting pupils with differing viewpoints and helping them to develop their own opinions, as well as enabling them to understand, appreciate and accept the views of others. We live in a society where conflict is not hard to find, whether it is in the playground, the pub on a Friday night, the planning committee, The House of Commons or the mountains of Bosnia. In listening to the belligerents in all these contexts you may be forgiven for believing that they have a slippery grip on reality. People have a way of speaking that is full of the conviction that what they say is fact.

These points are highly relevant to current political debate on morality and citizenship.

Sadly, most pupils leave school having never been asked to distinguish fact from non-fact, except perhaps in some very specialised contexts, such as evaluating historical evidence and testing scientific hypotheses. Surely such a fundamental distinction deserves more attention, not in the sense that pupils 'have to be taught', but in the sense that they should be asked to consider the issue. This activity is the most philosophical in the book because it begins to ask questions about the very nature of knowledge. As such it is one of the most challenging to use.

However there are far more instrumental reasons for considering the question of what is a fact. Many contemporary GCSE and A Level syllabuses make explicit reference to understanding values and attitudes, exploring issues and making decisions. Through examining the extent to which truth underpins statements and viewpoints, you give pupils a real grasp on the way in which values colour a person's view of the world.

This understanding is central to the big concept of decision making (see page 170).

Fact or Opinion?

Exemplar 1:

The future of Antarctica

Context

This particular lesson was used with top set Y9 classes who were undertaking group enquiry work into the Antarctic. It was therefore addressing paragraph 15 of the PoS. They were working with a range of questions relating to whether and how the continent should be protected. Pupils had been given a wide choice of finished product for the enquiry ranging from display work to a video news report, as long as the work was based around the issue of *'Protecting Antarctica'*. I felt that it was important that pupils understood and appreciated that different people would have different ideas on what should be done with this 'last wilderness', so that they could address the potential conflicts in their finished work.

The activity had the following purposes:
- to develop a more critical approach to information from interest groups through identifying the value positions behind statements;
- to provide an assessment opportunity for the higher level descriptors in the National Curriculum Orders.

In relation to the latter point, I felt that it was very important to really open up the Antarctic issue to scrutiny to make those levels accessible. The particular strands that I had in mind were:
- Level 6: *'...describe and offer explanations for different approaches to managing environments.'*;
- Level 7: *'...show understanding that many factors influence decisions made about places.'*;
- Level 8: *'...recognise the causes and consequences of environmental issues and show understanding of different approaches to tackling them.'*

The mention of 'different approaches' (Level 6), 'many factors influencing decisions' (Level 7) and 'causes and consequences of environmental issues' (Level 8), really invited the dissection of interest group statements.

Notice that these quotes relate strongly to the big concepts of planning, decision making and cause and effect (see pages 167 and 170).

Preparation

There is little physical preparation required, apart from duplicating the Resource sheet (FACT OR OPINION RESOURCE SHEET 1). It is worth noting that some of this was taken directly from the very popular series by Waugh & Bushell, which indicates how such resources can be adapted for very different purposes other from those originally intended. However, it was important to read through the material carefully myself to anticipate some of the issues that might arise as pupils did the task. I did not want to have to respond off-the-cuff. It was helpful for instance to consider what is meant by *'Antarctica is fragile'*. This process helped me to recall and review what I do know about Antarctica.

As pupils had already begun the enquiry in friendship groups of 5-6, these were kept the same, although for the first part of the activity, groups were subdivided into twos or threes.

Launching

No special activity was undertaken as the task was well embedded in the overall work that the class was doing. (However see Exemplar 2 and Afterthoughts for some possibilities.)

Instructions

1. Pupils were asked to work in pairs or threes within their larger groups.
2. Each pupil was given a viewpoints sheet (FACT OR OPINION RESOURCE SHEET 1) and asked to read through the statements carefully.
3. A few class questions were asked to make sure that some key vocabulary was understood, eg, exploit, superiority, resources, geology, krill. (For a less able class these could be on the board as well, or the resource could be re-written.)

> **Fact or Opinion?**
> **Exemplar 1:**
> **The future of Antarctica**

4. Working in pairs, pupils were asked to look carefully through all the different viewpoints and record them under one of two headings 'fact' and 'opinion' (no other help was given initially as the class was an able one). Pupils were allowed and even encouraged to split the statements into parts.

5. After about 15 minutes pupils were asked to compare their lists with others from their main group (of 6) and try to discuss/sort out any differences they might find.

Managing the activity

Some pupils thought very deeply and argued with each other; others agreed easily without much thought. The most important points were as follows:

- monitoring the pair-work was vital so that pupils could ask for help if they were unsure, as was the case with an activity that was totally new to them;
- however, it is important that the teacher does not interrupt at this stage—much useful discussion goes on between the pupils;
- some pupils naturally prefer to work alone and needed to be encouraged to compare their lists statement by statement. This is probably more of a feature of a high ability group;
- if groups seem to be in difficulty, simple questions can help such as: *'Why do you think that is a fact?' 'How do you know that is definitely a fact?'*

> *This may be a feature of different learning styles.*

The main issue in many of their questions was what do you do with those facts which are essentially a statement of opinion, eg, *'WWF believes that the minerals of Antarctica should not be exploited'*. It is a fact (probably) that WWF believes this, but the core of the statement is an opinion. This compares with those facts which are based on reasonable evidence, eg, *'Drilling in the 1970s found signs of oil'*. Some groups asked for help and others made their own decisions. Most saw from an early stage that there was some overlap. They began to see that, within the framework of the exercise, opinion was not by definition—bad, and fact—good.

Debriefing

The main aim of debriefing was to help pupils understand the processes behind the decisions they made, thus the following questions were used:

- *'How did you decide that something was a fact?'*
- *'How did you decide that something was an opinion?'*

> *These initial insights are very powerful and begin to question the very nature of geographical knowledge and its relationship to values.*

Their view was that facts and figures or evidence make something a fact, but it becomes an opinion when you make a judgement. They thought that opinions started with phrases such as *'I think'* or *'I feel'*. Because of the pressure of time I did not pursue this, although much more could have been said.

- *'Were some statements more difficult than others to classify?'*

Those where they could not decide whether or not they could take the 'facts' for granted.

- *'Why are there so many different viewpoints about what should be done with Antarctica?'*

They said because different people wanted different things, but they made no clear reference to values.

Follow-up

As this was only part of a much larger project, pupils were asked to keep their tables for future reference, but were reminded that their finished product had to include reference to differing viewpoints and how these could be accommodated.

Fact or Opinion?
Exemplar 1:
The future of Antarctica

Viewpoints

Task 1
What do people think about the future of Antarctica? Study the four viewpoints below. Choose **one** view that you support and **one** view that you disagree with. Explain your choices.

Task 2
Why do different views make conservation more difficult?

Our people have been fishing the Antarctic seas since the early twentieth century. No one owns these waters; they are here for anyone to use. We depend on fishing for our livelihood. What right have people to prevent us from making a living? Our country and our families benefit from our work. Don't stop us fishing; we will control our catches if everyone else does.

Fishermen

Environmentalists

Antarctica is the last wilderness on earth. Human activity in Antarctica should be banned, or at least carefully managed. The earth does not need to exploit this area for coal, oil, fish, etc. Antarctica is fragile—spoil it now and it will be lost forever. We must agree on how best to use the region. We support the idea of a World Wilderness Park.

The developed countries want to exploit the resources of Antarctica to keep their superiority over the rest of the world. What rights do they have to ravage the last area of true wilderness? Antarctica belongs to the world and not just to a group of rich and powerful countries. If the resources are to be used, they should benefit the whole world. The use of these resources should be carefully managed to prevent destruction of the Antarctic environment.

Politicians in the developing world

Scientists have been studying Antarctica since 1830. Today, scientists from a number of countries are researching into biology, geology, ice and climate. Many projects are proving to be useful to humanity. Research into climate is helping us to understand the world's changing weather. Pollution studies are providing information on the effects of human activities on climate and new resources are being discovered.

Scientists

Source: Waugh & Bushell: *Foundations of Geography.*

More viewpoints

**Fact or Opinion?
Exemplar 1:
The future of Antarctica**

Greenpeace

Greenpeace campaigns to protect Antarctica. It believes that there should not be any exploitation of the minerals in Antarctica. Greenpeace want a fifty-year ban on all mineral exploitation in Antarctica. Greenpeace supports the idea that Antarctica should be a 'World Park' that is protected.

Mining Companies

Many minerals have been discovered in Antarctica, and many areas still have to be explored. We believe that valuable resources will be found and that we should be allowed to mine them. We would try to be careful with the environment, and make the damage as little as possible. We think that politicians should make plans for Antarctica that allow minerals to be mined.

WWF

WWF believes that the minerals of Antarctica should not be exploited. They say that accidents often happen that cause pollution. For example, oil tankers can run aground, and spill their oil into the sea, killing a lot of wildlife, like birds and seals. All the pollution will also cause problems for whales, penguins, krill and fish. WWF supports the idea that Antarctica is made into a 'World Park'.

Oil Companies

Drilling in the 1970s found signs of oil off the Antarctic. Many oil companies are interested in the area. We understand the need to conserve the environment, but our industry has a good record of concern about the environment. The oil supplies we have now will not last forever, we need new ones. We should be allowed to drill for oil in Antarctica.

**Fact or Opinion?
Exemplar 2:
The Los Angeles riots**

Context

This was trialled with a middle band Y8 class, who were generally well motivated. It was part of a unit on North America (PoS paras 5a, b, c and d), but the exercise could very easily be used in work on urban geography. Pupils had studied migration and towards the end of the previous lesson we had watched a bit of news footage on the Los Angeles riots of 1993.

There was not a strong content rationale. I was influenced by the fact that the Y11s in the school are just not very questioning and have a very closed down view of what school is for, to the detriment of their performance in exams—they are not prepared to think much. So this lesson was an experiment and loaded towards achieving long term aims. I wanted to get them thinking.

Preparation

I had access to a variety of newspaper resources on the Los Angeles riots which followed the acquittal of the police officers who were accused of assaulting Rodney King. I chose one article because it really brought out the question of values, and another because it was short and factual. Because some pupils were not good readers, I decided to try to simplify the language and shorten the first piece (see FACT OR OPINION? RESOURCE SHEETS 2 and 3).

I constructed groups of three taking care to distribute the more able between groups.

Launching

I had thought about starting with the famous quote about *'lies, damned lies and statistics'*, but I thought that this was too ambitious. Instead I put up three statements on the board:

- *'Your room is untidy.'*
- *'You don't take enough care over your homework.'*
- *'You don't tell me/us about what goes on at school.'*

I asked whether their parent(s) ever said any of these things to them and asked them to put their hands up if the answer was *'Yes'* as we went through the questions one by one. About half put their hands up for the first statement, (pleasingly) only about a quarter for the second, and nearly three-quarters for the last one. I then asked them to put up their hands again if they disagreed with their parents on any of the statements. There were plenty of hands up, so I asked a few, in turn, why they disagreed. There were a few opinions about rooms, such as *'It is your own room, so you should decide'* and *'She wants it like the rest of the house'*. In relation to the last statement, several said that it was boring to tell their parents about school.

This is a bridging activity, endeavouring to use pupil experience as a foundation for learning.

I summed up by pointing out that in each case there was only one bedroom, but for some of the class there were different opinions about what it was like. In fairness, I felt that they were a little confused at this point and I hope that I can improve on this start in future.

Can we avoid confusion entirely when the change we seek is so fundamental?

Instructions

1. The pupils were put in threes. I think that pairs would work just as well in many cases.
2. They were asked to read the text through (FACT OR OPINION? RESOURCE SHEET 2). I told them that the woman who had written it clearly lived in a wealthy part of LA. I said they could ask questions in a few minutes if there were any things that they did not understand. I was really pleased that they did. Of course they asked what a baby shower was—I have no

idea and told them so. They also asked about 'deferentially', 'curfew', 'Reagan', 'haves' and 'have-nots'. I turned all these questions back to the class and in every case someone answered.

3. I told them to look carefully at the 10 underlined sections and decide whether they were fact or just an opinion. I did not try to define them. I told them they could split the passages if one part was fact and one part opinion. I also said that they could invent new headings or categories if they felt that some bits were neither fact nor opinion. We did the first one together. They all agreed that this was a fact.

Managing the activity

I tried to stand back, but it was obvious that I needed to help some groups. The worst aspect was that one group of more able pupils was whizzing through the 10 deciding that they were all facts. I took them back to number 4, *'Nobody who doesn't live there would ever be caught dead going there'*. I pulled out the words nobody and ever and said, *'Are you sure that that is a fact—nobody, ever?'* Two of them started to rethink, but one boy stuck to his opinion and said that you know what it means. I suggested that he could call that a new category and left it at that. They did slow down.

I was also amazed (and horrified) to find that some groups were happy to accept number 7 as a fact, *'It's black people's own fault they're in the trouble they're in. Look how well the Koreans do.'* This was definitely one of the hardest lessons that I have taught because there were so many occasions when I did not know what to do.

Those that finished first were asked to go back and think carefully about any extra categories. I only waited till about half the groups had done all 10 before calling a halt. One group, which had argued a lot had only got as far as number 4.

Debriefing

I had been very careful to leave 15 minutes of a 50-minute lesson to discuss the activity. In the end it was not enough and I did not use the second source at all.

Basically what happened as we went through each one was that they got less and less certain about many of the statements and about facts—and so did I! Some really promising comments were made such as *'Facts can be proved'* and *'Some things are probably true but you cannot be sure'*.

I felt very strongly the need to sum up the lesson, for fear of leaving them confused. So I said that we seemed to agree that *'the city is burning'* is a fact and blaming the blacks is an opinion (and in my view unjustified). Before I could go any further one of the brightest boys said, *'If you put "I think" in front of an opinion it becomes a fact.'* At first I did not understand, but he meant that if you have an opinion but you start by saying *'I think'* or *'I feel'* it is a fact that it is your thought or feeling and somehow this is more acceptable. Some of the class were very restless by this stage, so I hurriedly reminded them that many of them thought that their parents were wrong in thinking that they had untidy bedrooms and this was just a difference of opinion.

I was left feeling half excited because of the potential for a stunning lesson, but frustrated because I had not planned it carefully enough and because many of the pupils did not get the point.

Fact or Opinion? Exemplar 2: The Los Angeles riots

*This is a fine example of developing a **community of enquiry**—pupils both ask and answer the questions to clarify the information available.*

Differentiation by teacher support?

This section exemplifies the task faced in using Thinking Through Geography activities—you face becoming a novice again because you have changed the rules (see pages 173–174).

Differentiation by outcome.

Fact or Opinion? Exemplar 2: The Los Angeles riots

Extract one: inspired by an article 'Fear and loathing in Hollywood' by Cynthia Heimel in the Independent on Sunday.

On the first day of the LA riots when thousands of fires raged and most of Los Angeles resembled Beirut, a bunch of women gathered for a baby shower given by one of the most famous movie stars at her most fabulous home. Everyone was in peach, mint or white. Everyone wore the palest ivory stockings. They sat under umbrellas while little tea sandwiches and scones were served deferentially by Mexican women.

Then the housekeeper appeared. 'Ma'am,' she said, 'The city is burning. People are getting killed. There's gonna be a curfew.'

South Central Los Angeles takes up about one-quarter of the city. Nobody who doesn't live there would ever be caught dead going there. Nobody who does live there ever leaves except to go to wait on rich people. Before Wednesday affluent Los Angeles denied the existence of South Central Los Angeles. The gulf between the haves and the have-nots is terrifying; the haves enjoy the inflated salaries of the entertainment industry; the have-nots subsist on minimum wage or welfare.

During the curfew we watched (on TV) the looting and fires spread to middle-class neighbourhoods. That's when people got scared.

'Oh my God, Sammy's camera repair!' said a screenwriter. 'They've got my Nikon there. Shi....'

'What if the tailor shop that's redoing my dress for the wedding burns down?', asked an actress.

During the curfew I discovered ugly things about people I thought I knew.

'It's black people's own fault they're in the trouble they're in. Look how well the Koreans do', said an animator.

'I feel like I should go up and apologise to black people,' said Paula, a musician. 'This has been coming on for so long. Our government is so unresponsive. The Rodney King ruling just lit a match. This country isn't working.'

'We should just find Reagan and give him to the rioters,' said Harriet, a journalist. 'Isn't it all his fault? His whole message to poor people was "Screw you, we're all getting rich as we can, and some money might trickle down if you're lucky. If not, tough".'

During the curfew, we had nothing to do but watch TV and see our city burn. And think.

Extract two

Fact or Opinion?

Exemplar 2:

The Los Angeles riots

US blacks: the facts

Fifty-three per cent of blacks believe African Americans are less intelligent than whites; 51 per cent believe they are less patriotic; 56 per cent believe they are more violence-prone; 62 per cent believe they are 'more likely to live off welfare' and less likely to 'prefer to be self-supporting'.

From a 1990 survey by the University of Chicago's National Opinion Research Center.

◆ **Black males have the lowest life-expectancy of any group in the United States.** Their unemployment rate is more than twice that of white males; even black men with college degrees are three times more likely to be unemployed than their white counterparts.

About one in four black men between the ages of 20 and 29 is behind bars. Blacks receive longer prison sentences than whites who have committed the same crimes.

◆ **Suicide is the third leading cause of death for young black males.** Since 1960, suicide rates for young blacks have nearly tripled, and doubled for black females. While suicide among whites increases with age, it is a peculiarly youthful phenomenon among blacks. Many black males die prematurely from 12 major preventable diseases.

◆ **Nearly one-third of all black families in America live below the poverty line.** Half of all black children are born in poverty and will spend all their youth growing up in poor families.

From a 1991 report of the 21st Century Commission on African-American Males.

Fact or Opinion?
Exemplar 3:
Nature's numbers

This demonstrates the explicit exam result orientation of all the Thinking Through Geography teachers.

Context

The target group for this exemplar was a Y12 A Level group. The special purpose related to the 16-19 A Level: People and Environmental Perspectives. In their essays, students tend to have problems with understanding issues and values, which can come up specifically in the title or be implicit. They don't do well if they write a one-sided essay. I wanted to highlight the relationship between standpoints, values, evidence and scientific certainty.

Preparation

The lesson is based on a BBC2 'Horizon' programme, *Nature's Numbers*, which continues to be an outstanding resource for teaching. Being able to show the programme is not essential, but is clearly an advantage. In this lesson the students watched the video and had to keep stopping it to transcribe, which was time consuming. I had watched it several times. Subsequently chunks of the programme have now been transcribed and slightly edited so that the students can focus on the task in hand. This is time consuming.

The other important facet of preparation is becoming familiar with the relationship between scientific evidence and theory. A useful, but possibly oversimplified, representation of this is to say that in ecology, at least, the greatest certainty is found at small scales, but as scales increase so does uncertainty and the tendency to speculate and theorise.

Launching

This was straightforward and was basically an appeal to their ambition to do well in the exams. Understanding the geographical issues was not enough; they also needed to understand what people thought and why.

I used atlases to identify the area featured in the programme: part of eastern Bolivia, that borders onto Amazonian Brazil.

Instructions

These are given on the resource sheet (FACT OR OPINION? RESOURCE SHEETS 4 and 5). You need to explain that the theorists are mainly academics from the United States.

Managing the activity

Differentiation by group work and teacher support is still important at A Level.

Reassurance was the key here. Some of the less accomplished students were struggling, but they were helped by the brighter ones and me. I encouraged them to consider the text in sentences, otherwise they might go too slowly.

They did not finish in the time available during the lesson, but they were now fairly confident of what to do, so they finished it in their own time.

I tried to ensure that they did not classify all the statements of the RAP (rapid assessment programme) team as opinion. I wanted the pattern to emerge that there was some evidence or fact about species at the local scale. However at the world scale of theorising about extinction, the same evidence used by different people could lead to opposing conclusions.

Debriefing

This took place during the following lesson and was simply stimulated by talking through their written work. The following points emerged:
- they had enjoyed the activity;
- different scientists say different things based on the same available data;

- people who work on the ground are more concerned with action, place more value on the aesthetic value of species and environments, and react more emotionally;
- theorists speculate more and are more influenced by political values—they tend to fail to see the trees for the wood (they undervalue the particular);
- much debate about conservation takes place without adequate facts, although this is less so in Britain and other developed countries where there is more research and possibly less to research because so much has gone already;
- we often fail to distinguish between fact and opinion—but scientists are also guilty of this;
- pressure groups tend to be very selective about the 'facts' that they draw upon to support their case;
- politicians are more concerned with economic development than with conservation because of the need for jobs;
- research and technology change what facts are over time—opinions can become facts if proved, and facts can be disproved.

Students were a little confused about the dividing lines between fact and opinion and about evidence. However they seemed much more willing to question sources and received wisdom, a trend which has snowballed over time.

Fact or Opinion?
Exemplar 3:
Nature's numbers

This really highlights the significance of values.

This is transfer (see page 162).

This is a tremendous list.

Fact or Opinion strategies can really begin to turn students' minds because they question the nature of knowledge.

Fact or Opinion?

Exemplar 3:

Nature's numbers

The case of the Park Noel Kempff Mercado, Bolivia

Instructions

The extracts are taken from or adapted from a BBC2 Horizon programme *Nature's Numbers*. The programme looks at species conservation at two scales: firstly, theories about extinction of species at the global scale, and secondly, conservation of species in the Park Noel Kempff Mercado in Bolivia, which has a wide variety of habitats including dry grassland and rainforest, and was established to conserve species. The programme follows in particular a rapid assessment programme (RAP) team, funded by a wildlife charity, who spend six weeks in the area in order to make recommendations to the government.

Task 1

Go through the quotes and decide what parts are fact and what parts are opinion. Be prepared to go back and change your mind. You don't have to work on the parts in bold, but do read them as they are important to the overall understanding. You are free to develop new categories beyond 'fact' and 'opinion'.

Task 2

What patterns emerge from the analysis?

Task 3

What value positions can you match up with the different standpoints on the conservation of species?

Task 4

How might the issues surrounding conservation be different in Britain?

The case of the Park Noel Kempff Mercado, Bolivia

Fact or Opinion? Exemplar 3: Nature's numbers

Quotes

Theorist: *'If you lose half of the forest in an area you lose 15% of the species that it contains'.*
Theorist: *'One of the problems with these big numbers that get banded about is that there are often exaggerations. We have no idea how many species there are in the world and we have no idea how many are becoming extinct each year.'*
Programme: *'The park is half the size of Northern Ireland.'*
RAP team member: *'We flew over the area to identify the critical areas that we should see during our 4 weeks of intensive surveying. We needed hard data. If there's no data on species at all on any area under threat, no group has any data at all to fight developments.'*
RAP team member: *'We are keen to find marker species- these provide a measure of the park's bio-diversity.'*
RAP team member: *'I hate killing it* (as he lethally injects a Smooth Fronted Cayman), *because it is a big animal, but it will be good for science in Bolivia. They don't have specimens in their collections and if they cannot identify the species they won't have time to monitor their populations.'*

To get a global picture of what is happening ecologists turn to theory. All the theory is based on experiments on two small mangrove islands off the Florida coast. All the animal species were exterminated on the two islands and then they were allowed to recolonise naturally. The larger island got more species than the smaller one. The number of species fluctuated somewhat on both islands as species came and went, but the number of species remained fairly constant. This led to the theory about species-area relationship. As you reduce the area, fewer individuals can live there, so in natural fluctuations the number can go to zero more easily.

Scientific journalist: *'There has been a tendency by at least some to use the species area curve for their political ends with the implication that you need to cease all development world-wide. It's really been an attempt to elevate a rather Quixotic political crusade to a level of scientific imperative.'*

Continued...

Fact or Opinion?
Exemplar 3:
Nature's numbers

Scientific journalist: 'You should not use the species area curve to predict what would happen on the mainland, because it has never been tested on islands of forest.'
US politician: 'What we need are facts—the stuff that science is made of.'
RAP team member: 'There's a beautiful large carnivorous frog that's really scarce in the dry forest.'

With 10 days left of the survey period the mammal specialist is surveying bats in just a small area of the park.

'Many species she caught are new to the species list of Bolivia. Nowhere in Bolivia has a complete species list. She could not identify all the bats she caught. Without knowing how many species there are it is hard to know how many are being lost.'
Theorist: 'Anecdotal evidence just does not meet the test of scientific validity. The reason we do a lot of research is to provide a scientific basis. Looking out of the window is not good enough. One hundred anecdotes are not better than one anecdote.'
Programme: 'There is a unique forest/grassland area outside the park, the Cerrado. Many local people are hostile towards the scientists because they do not want more restrictions on local industries, which provide jobs in a poor rural area.'
RAP team member: 'There are some interesting species that don't seem to be here, particularly several species of monkey that we are pretty sure should be here, but there's something missing in the environment which they require. I do think that there's a crisis of extinction—parts of the Cerrado here are getting on the edge, starting to go extinct.'
Politician (Malaysian Prime Minister): 'To say just in case something is there we must save everything—that is just not on.'
RAP team member: 'I'm particularly excited about what may be a new species of frog in one of my favourite groups.'

Before they flew out the team had to agree on their recommendations to the park management:

Continued...

> **RAP team member:** 'About half the expected species are here. The most interesting ones were found in the dry habitats, the Cerrado in particular. It would be nice to get that area under the control of the park authorities, rather than controlled from outside the park.'

> **RAP team member:** 'What really struck me after visiting the dry area and seeing what they are cutting now, they are going after the big beautiful forest with maybe 40–50% of the big tree species and that's why I would really push for extending the park down to the Tarvo River. The park is threatened by development on three sides—logging, cattle ranching and growing soya beans.'

> **Theorist:** 'The species extinction question is another in a long line of social and scientific questions that many have believed is too important to demand ordinary scientific proofs for. But time after time when there is time to gather the data, it turns out that what people felt in their gut was not validated by the scientific evidence.'

> **Theorist:** 'In ecology, as in medicine, a false positive (that is believing something may be happening when it is not actually happening) is something that can be corrected with further research. But a false negative (saying that something is not ongoing) such as extinctions which we observe or a serious disease, can be dangerous.'

Fact or Opinion? Exemplar 3: Nature's numbers

This one park has been surveyed and the RAP will continue to work on the small local scale, feeding fragments of information into the abstractions of global ecological theory.

> **RAP team member:** 'It's not bad, in fact it's quite good, to theorise about a lot of these things but the reality is that we've got to do something that works—that actually protects something down here. But no matter how many beautiful theories there may be they don't easily translate into actually getting something protected on the ground.'

In October 1995, the Park Noel Kempff Mercado was extended by 135,000 hectares to include areas of dry forest. The Cerrado was not included.

END

Fact or Opinion?: Adapting the strategy

Clearly this is a very adaptable strategy, because there are so many pieces of text that can be used. However, some texts are better then others. A good 'type' of text is one in which a variety of people are giving their opinions about the same area or issue. Statements by politicians or pressure groups are a good starting point. Many textbooks have 'talking heads' or cartoons with speech bubbles and these can be a good source.

In preparing the resource it may be helpful to simplify it and/or to underline specific parts that you want analysed, as in the Los Angeles example (Exemplar 2).

Afterthoughts

This is the sort of activity that can be hard to sell to colleagues, partly because it is difficult to manage and partly because they don't see the point. Its immediate payoff may be negligible, especially in terms of content. The payoff comes in the longer run and, like politicians, perhaps we have become short termists.

It is evident that some students really enjoyed doing ***Fact or Opinion*** exercises, others were irritated. They implied that they thought it was pointless, although this did not occur with the A Level group who could see the relevance to exams. I think these reactions are much to do with learning styles: those who like to question and think were in their element, and those who like learning to be simple, clear-cut and unproblematic were suffering. One can make a good case for the view that just because they don't like it does not mean that they should not do it.

At the time of writing, the media and politicians are much exercised about morality. It seems to us that ***Fact or Opinion*** has more to say about teaching about morality than any new set of commandments for schools on the subject.

Classification

Rationale

Classifying is one of the most fundamental cognitive skills, as can be seen from the description of the concept of classification (CLASSIFICATION RESOURCE SHEET 1). In geography, if you have strong categories for dealing with information in topics and case studies, you have a way of processing data that begins to transform the subject from an incoherent jumble to a view of the world. Classifying can be seen as a most basic tool for forming ideas about the world. With this advantage students can see the 'big pictures' in the subject.

Of key importance in **Classification** is developing the ability to recognise **characteristics**, which are the distinguishing attributes used to group objects or events. A really able student can implicitly place an order on the importance of characteristics of a phenomenon. We are aiming to nudge more students in that direction. So for example when they next see a report on an earthquake on the TV news they make greater sense of parts of the report. There could be a shot of a trained dog looking for survivors—yes they might think *'Oh! what a clever dog— I like dogs!'*, they might also respond, *'That is one of the ways in which communities can deal with the immediate aftermath of a disaster'*. In the first case, the dominant characteristics perceived are 'nice cuddly animal'.

> *This would constitute an example of transfer (see page 162).*

On the whole, students can classify well in their everyday life. The whole point of these activities is that this process becomes more conscious, informed and sophisticated. Students can become better human information processors.

> *This is metacognition at work (see page 159).*

Classification
Thinking skills: introduction

Thinking skills: introduction to classification

Many newspapers have 'Classified' sections where people advertise their goods and services for sale.

Task 1

Look at these adverts from the 'classified' section of a local newspaper.

(a) Carefully read the adverts and headings below.

(b) Using these headings, *classify* the adverts under the *correct* heading.

(c) Write the advert's number under each heading.

1.	OVAL CLUSTER 18 Carat Ring, Sapphire with 14 Diamonds surround. £550 o.n.o.	7.	GOLD NECKLACE. 20" chain, 18 carat gold, unwanted gift, £35 o.n.o.
2.	HI-FI SYSTEM Sony, silver, excluding tuner with cabinet. £80. o.n.o.	8.	HOTPOINT FRIDGE FREEZER almond colour, immaculate condition. £80 o.n.o.
3.	LEC FRIDGE/FREEZER up-right, cream coloured, 5ft. Perfect working order. £80. o.n.o.	9.	FLYMO GARDEN vac and strimmer. Less than half price. £60 the pair, good condition.
4.	CAR DOOR SPEAKERS Pioneer, 4" TS 1007, excellent sound. £15.	10.	RABBIT HUTCH joiner-made from waterproof ply, very good condition, large, separate bedroom. £30.
5.	NEWFOUNDLAND PUPPIES excellent pedigree, lovely character, home bred. Ready 1st March.	11.	LAWN TURF 3 grades, cheap prices. Access and Visa accepted. Wardley.
6.	ALUMINIUM GREENHOUSE dismantled 7 x 6 feet, reasonable condition. £38.		

PETS	GARDENING
MUSIC	**JEWELLERY**
FRIDGES	

Thinking skills: introduction to classification

Classification
Thinking skills: introduction

Task 2

(a) Read the adverts numbered 1 to 11 below.

(b) Try to come up with 4 suitable headings to classify them all into.

(c) Write your chosen headings at the bottom of the sheet.

1.	ELECTRIC ORGAN Viscount, double keyboard, roll-top and stool. £125.	7.	DRUMS Premier APK, 5 piece kit with a Premier 2000 snare. Includes symbols and stands. £350 o.n.o.
2.	SKIS 207cm. Atomic RS Bionic, good condition. Marker Rotamat bindings. 1988, hardly used. £170.	8.	HASSELBLAD MEDIUM FORMAT CAMERA two A12 film backs, 80mm lens, good condition. £850.
3.	FULL SET GOLF CLUBS Ping Eye 2 Plus Irons, 3 metal woods, putter, bag and trolley. £280.	9.	ROWI PROFESSIONAL 2 tier slide projector stand. £15. Boxed zoom lens. £35 o.n.o.
4.	WHITE DINING TABLE, six chairs, modern IKEA, excellent condition. £325 o.n.o.	10.	WALL MOUNTED CABINETS solid oak. £50 each, good condition.
5.	GOLD DRALON three piece suite with reclining chair. Very good condition. £100 o.n.o.	11.	WEIDER HOME GYM Resistance bands. Unwanted Xmas gift. £80.
6.	SOFA BED pale green and grey, excellent condition. £50.		

HEADINGS:

1.	2.
3.	4.

Classification Resource Sheet 1   *Thinking Through Geography*

Classification Exemplar 1:

The great Kanto earthquake, Tokyo, 1923

Context

This exercise is suitable for use at both Key Stage 3 and Key Stage 4, and was trialled with mixed ability Y11 classes. It was introduced half way through a unit of work on natural hazards, once the students had a firm grasp of plate tectonics, the structure of volcanoes and the cause and effects of volcanic eruptions. At this stage, the students had not studied the human response to such natural disasters and this exercise was designed to encourage them to do so. It was also the intention that through using collaborative group work all abilities would benefit.

Preparation

Preparation for the activity is vital. The following is a good checklist:

1. If possible, print copies of CLASSIFICATION RESOURCE SHEET 2 on different coloured paper, as this makes the task of sorting the statements into envelopes easier. It also prevents the students getting their statements mixed up with those of other groups, during and after the lesson.

2. Cut up the RESOURCE SHEET and place the statements into envelopes. This saves a lot of classroom time and makes the exercise easier to manage.

3. If you have a more able class, you can increase the difficulty of the activity by removing the headings under 'Human response' and devise new instructions for tasks 2 and 3 (CLASSIFICATION RESOURCE SHEET 3).

4. Arrange the classroom so that groups of two or three can work on the activity together.

5. Carefully plan your groups in advance, to ensure that each group represents the range of abilities in the class.

6. Prepare an OHT of CLASSIFICATION RESOURCE SHEET 3 to aid instruction.

Launching

In order to engage interest in the activity, familiarise the students with the technique of **Classification**. This can be done in various ways: for example by asking students to classify objects under the headings of animal, vegetable or mineral, or countries into continents, etc. This will also serve to increase their confidence. Alternatively you could use the starter activity (CLASSIFICATION RESOURCE SHEET 1). Interest can also be engaged by supplying the students with visual stimuli, such as a video clip or a black and white print, showing the dramatic effects of an earthquake. (CD ROMs will be an excellent source for this.)

This bridges into the activity.

Instructions

1. After introducing the activity, distribute the envelopes containing the statements.

2. First instruct the students to sort the statements in numerical order, to check that each group has a full set.

3. As a class, read through each statement and explain any difficult vocabulary. A more able group can just read through themselves and be given a chance to ask for clarification.

Notice the responsibility for doing this has been with students in many exemplars.

4. Distribute CLASSIFICATION RESOURCE SHEET 3. Because a single question might present a barrier to the less able in the class, this sheet breaks down the overall activity into a series of discrete tasks, so that students are quite clear about what is expected of them. Ample scope is still left for a high level response to task 4.

This is careful scaffolding.

5. Talk through causes first, then effects and, finally, human response to make sure that they are understood. Instruct students to sort the

statements under the three headings of causes, effects and human response (task 2). Do two examples as a class.

6. Once the sorting has been completed, ask selected groups to talk about their results to the rest of the class. (Encourage students to quote the number of each statement when discussing their classification decisions, so that the information can be handled quickly and easily by the teacher and by the rest of the class. Good discussion will also arise when students disagree on the classification of some statements.)

7. Once there is a general consensus, introduce and explain task 3. With a more confident class, the students can devise their own categories for the human response.

8. Attention should be drawn to the sub-classification headings provided in the table on CLASSIFICATION RESOURCE SHEET 3. Do 2 examples as a class (use the OHT).

9. Ask students to record their work in the table for each task as they go along.

10. Once the table is complete, collect the statements and debrief.

11. Introduce and explain task 4. Encourage students to work independently throughout this task.

Classification Exemplar 1: The great Kanto earthquake, Tokyo, 1923

Managing the Activity

Allow sufficient time for students to classify the statements in tasks 2 and 3. Clearly the time allowed will depend on the ability of the students involved—the whole activity can take from 2 to 4 lessons to complete. However, it is vital that clear time limits be imposed and adhered to, so that pace is maintained and opportunity is given to students to report back. As often as possible, facilitate and motivate students who may struggle. Organising groupings in advance should cut down on the number of obstacles encountered. However, if a group is clearly floundering, sit with them, read the statements to them and help them to focus their ideas. If the activity is going to run over several lessons, enough time must be left at the end of each to discuss what the students have achieved so far, and to set targets for the next lesson.

Differentiation by teacher support.

Debriefing

This is perhaps the most difficult part of the activity, but, with practice, it does become easier for both teacher and students. Encourage the students to think about **how** they completed the activity and aim to identify other areas where the knowledge gained, concepts established, and processes utilised could be relevant.

Transfer.

Ask each group to describe how they classified the information, the cause of any disagreements that arose in relation to the classification, and how these were resolved.

- Ask students what they have learnt from the exercise. Concentrate not only on the skill of classification, but also on that of piecing together disjointed information to produce a coherent report.

- Discuss how they tried to analyse the different response strategies and how they decided what human responses were most effective in saving life.

- Explore connections to other contexts. Make the students aware of **Classification** in everyday life and how it is based on shared characteristics, eg, the classification of music (jazz, pop, rock), of books (thrillers, romance, children's), of football teams (into divisions), of firms in the *Yellow Pages*, etc.

More transfer.

Thinking Through Geography

Classification Exemplar 1:

The great Kanto earthquake, Tokyo, 1923

- Discuss how they ranked the responses to the earthquake. Examine how we use the skill of prioritisation every day (in deciding what to take on holiday, time management in relation to deadlines, etc). Encourage the students to think of their own examples.

Follow-up

Encourage students to produce a detailed report on the causes, effects and responses to the great Kanto earthquake (Task 4). Ask them to structure their paragraphs according to the *Classification* headings and sub-headings, making sure that they try to: incorporate an explanation for the effects; justify the response measures taken; explain which of these measures they think would be the most effective in saving lives.

It may be a good idea to supply low ability students with a writing frame (see page 81) to help them structure their ideas, eg,

The earthquake happened because....

The effects on people were...,.

The effects on buildings were....

I think that these effects were very bad because..., etc.

However it is structured, students must understand the importance of writing the report in their own words. If you are not careful they will copy down the statements without much thought and interpretation.

Classification

Classification Exemplar 1:

The great Kanto earthquake, Tokyo, 1923

Statements

Japan gets about 5000 tremors a year. There are three a month in Tokyo that can be felt. The following statements are about the causes of, effects of and human responses to the great Kanto earthquake which happened in Tokyo on the 1st September, 1923 at 11.58 am.

1.	Modern skyscrapers are now built with steel frames that can sway during an earthquake.
2.	The harbour was flooded by a Tsunami (a tidal wave caused by the earthquake).
3.	Main road bridges have been improved and strengthened.
4.	100,000 people died in Tokyo and 40,000 in Yokohama.
5.	Schools do regular earthquake drills with their pupils.
6.	Many people died when their feet got stuck in melting tarmac.
7.	Many households have earthquake kits—bottled water, rice, radio and fire extinguishers.
8.	People are advised not to store things on high shelves.
9.	People are now advised to switch off ovens and gas stoves during an earthquake.
10.	Instruments are used to measure earth movements. The next earthquake is predicted for 2020.
11.	Many fires started as stoves exploded and gas mains were broken. These fires lasted 2 days.
12.	Some buildings have built-in computer controlled cable tensioning systems.
13.	The Shirahige-Higashi apartment complex was built as a firebreak.
14.	Japan lies on the boundary of the Eurasian Plate and stresses build up.
15.	A rescue and emergency centre with a heliport has been established at an old air base.
16.	543 hectares of housing have been strengthened and fire proofed by the city authorities.

Continued...

Classification Exemplar 1:

The great Kanto earthquake, Tokyo, 1923

Statements continued

17.	Fire breaks have been built by demolishing buildings.
18.	The city authorities promise to give people a few hours warning of a major earthquake.
19.	Buildings have inner and outer walls to strengthen them.
20.	The city put an earthquake plan together in 1983. It has cost a lot of money.
21.	Many modern buildings have shock-absorbers built into them.
22.	Emergency water tanks and generators have been installed in each district.
23.	There had not been a major earthquake in Tokyo since 1853.
24.	More open spaces have been created by reclaiming land and knocking down buildings.
25.	700,000 homes and 9,000 factories were destroyed. Fires burnt 66% of the city.
26.	The earthquake measured 8.2 on the Richter Scale.
27.	The Pacific Plate and Philippines Plate are being subducted under the Eurasian Plate.
28.	The houses were wooden and caught fire quickly. There was no open space between them, so the fire spread.
29.	Many power cables fell and two-thirds of Tokyo was destroyed.
30.	Every September 1st is Japan's 'Disaster Day' and people practise earthquake drills.
31.	Many people died by breathing in smoke from the fires. Others were trampled to death on a bridge.
32.	The epicentre was 80 km south of Tokyo. It took 44 seconds for the shockwaves to hit Tokyo.

Causes, Effects and Responses

Classification Exemplar 1: The great Kanto earthquake, Tokyo, 1923

Task 1: Carefully read through the statements in the envelope provided.

Task 2: Classify the statements into 3 piles: (i) Causes statements (ii) Effects statements and (iii) Human response statements.

Task 3: Further classify these piles of statements using the headings given below. After discussion, use this information to complete the table. Wherever possible, write up the information in your own words.

Task 4: Using all of this information, write a detailed report about the 1923 great Kanto earthquake in your book. Make sure that you also try to:

(i) Explain why earthquakes happen at plate boundaries.

(ii) Explain why the effects were so bad.

(iii) Justify the human response. Why were these strategies used?

Which do you think are the most effective strategies in saving lives? Why?

Causes of the earthquake	Effects of the earthquake (immediate)	Human response
Why did the earthquake happen?	Effects on people	Strategies to educate the population about earthquakes.
		Strategies to deal with the immediate effects of an earthquake.
		Strategies to improve transport links.
		Strategies to improve buildings in Tokyo.
What was the strength and why was it so powerful?	Effects on buildings in Tokyo.	
		Strategies to prevent fires spreading.
		Strategies to predict future earthquakes.

Classification Exemplar 2: The response to Hurricane Gloria, USA

The Context

This exercise is suitable for use at both Key Stage 3 and Key Stage 4 and was trialled with mixed ability year 8 and 9 classes. It was introduced halfway through a unit of work on weather, once pupils had a basic grasp of the cause and effects of hurricanes. At this stage, the pupils had not studied the human response to such extreme weather and this exercise was designed to encourage them to do so. It will be obvious that the subject context is similar to the first exemplar on earthquakes and this gives a great opportunity to work on transfer.

Preparation

1. Arrange the classroom so that groups of two, three or four can work on the activity together.
2. Carefully plan your groups in advance, to ensure that each group represents the range of ability in the class.
3. Prepare an OHT of the resource sheets (CLASSIFICATION RESOURCE SHEETS 4 and 5).
4. You may need to secure a supply of red, green and blue pencils, if your pupils are unlikely to have their own.

Launching

In order to engage interest in the activity, familiarise the pupils with the technique of *Classification*—refer to details in Exemplar 1. This will stimulate good discussion work and should help to build confidence. Visual stimuli (for example, a video clip showing the dramatic effects of a hurricane) may also prove useful in arousing interest.

Instructions

1. After introducing the activity, distribute CLASSIFICATION RESOURCE SHEETS 4.
2. As a class, read through the newspaper article on the response to Hurricane Gloria and clarify any difficult vocabulary.
3. Draw the pupils' attention to CLASSIFICATION RESOURCE SHEETS 5. Explain the aims of the activity and the meaning of the words authorities, businesses and individuals.
4. Instruct pupils to shade the three headings in the table.
5. Using an OHT of the newspaper article, underline a few sentences as a class, to reinforce pupils' understanding of the activity.
6. Instruct the pupils to write up this information in the boxes on CLASSIFICATION RESOURCE SHEETS 5. (This can be done for homework.)
7. Once the table is complete, ask each group to outline some of their choices to the class.
8. There will certainly be some disagreement between groups, so encourage all pupils to justify their classification choice.
9. Debrief the activity.

Managing the activity

Allow adequate time for pupils to identify and classify the different responses. Clearly the time allowed will depend on the ability of the pupils involved, and the activity can take from 2 to 4 lessons to complete. However, it is vital that clear time limits be imposed and adhered to, so that pace is maintained and opportunity is given to pupils to report back. As often as possible, facilitate and motivate pupils who may struggle. Organising groupings in advance should cut down on the number of obstacles encountered. However, if a group is clearly floundering, sit with them, read the newspaper article with them, support them in the identification and classification of the different responses.

Debriefing

Encourage the pupils to think about **how** they completed the activity and aim to identify other areas where the knowledge gained, concepts established and processes utilised could be relevant.

- Ask each group how they identified the different response strategies.
- Ask each group to describe how they classified these responses, the cause of any disagreements that arose in relation to such classification and how a final decision was reached.
- Ask them what they have learnt from the exercise.
- Also discuss connections to other contexts. Make the pupils aware of classification in everyday life and how it is based on shared characteristics, eg. the classification of music (jazz, pop, rock), of books (thrillers, romance, children's), etc.
- Discuss how they ranked the responses to the hurricane. If you have covered another natural hazard or even used the earthquake exercise in the first exemplar you should try to make connections to the human response in that context, as there are many parallels. Examine how we use the skill of prioritisation every day (in deciding what to take on holiday, time management in relation to deadlines, etc). Encourage the pupils to think of their own examples.

Follow-up

Instruct the pupils to produce a report on the responses of authorities, businesses and individuals to Hurricane Gloria. Make it clear that they not only have to **describe** the different responses to the hurricane, but also try to **explain** them. Encourage pupils to write about which responses they think are the most effective in saving lives. The more able pupils could also sub-classify the action taken by authorities into those taken by the military, the police, civil and transport authorities.

It may be a good idea to supply low ability pupils with a writing frame to help them structure their ideas, eg,

The authorities reacted by....

Businesses responded by....

Individuals decided to....

I think the best response was..., etc.

Classification

Exemplar 2:

The response to Hurricane Gloria, USA

This task connects very clearly to the NC level descriptors.

Classification Exemplar 2:
The response to Hurricane Gloria, USA

Hurricane Gloria hits the U.S.A.

Some 300,000 Americans fled the coastal areas as Hurricane Gloria wrecked the Eastern Seaboard yesterday. The beginning of what was described as "the storm of the century" virtually shut down New York, although it hardly touched the city as it died out in Connecticut.

In Atlantic City, New Jersey, the casinos closed for the first time. In New York, the stock exchanges closed and the World Trade Centre, which was swaying under the force of the winds, was also shut down. The torch of the statue of liberty, which had been sitting outside a workshop at the statue's base, was moved indoors.

United Nations staff members who reported for work were given the day off, and a big demonstration by Polish exiles stopped due to heavy rain.

Radio bulletins warned New Yorkers not to go out unless they had to, and not to drive. The streets were empty and most shops were closed with their plate glass windows covered in tape to prevent them from shattering.

New York's Mayor, Ed Koch, had asked residents of Staten Island and Coney Island to evacuate to higher ground and 15 shelters were set up, but Gloria gave New York City a miss, destroying the outer shore along the east coast and then smashing into the eastern end of Long Island and New England. Power lines were damaged; half of Long Island was without electricity last night. There was heavy flooding and all the main highways were closed due to fallen trees and large branches.

The powerful waves blew over trees and resort boardwalks. Swells of water, 10 to 12 feet above normal, cut off roads into New Jersey's barrier islands and police blockaded all other roads to the islands.

Radio and television stations dropped their regular programmes to issue warnings, which included "stay away from grandfather clocks which could start rocking and fall".

The commuter rail service from New York to its Connecticut suburbs was suspended as trees and power lines piled up on tracks, and flights at the major

east coast airports, including Washington's National Airport and Kennedy Airport, New York, were cancelled.

The only parts seriously damaged were the rich, exclusive buildings in the Hamptons and along the Connecticut shore. Property damage was reported to be heavy, but considerably less than had been expected.

The Navy recalled its ships from exercises off the coast to the naval bases such as Annapolis.

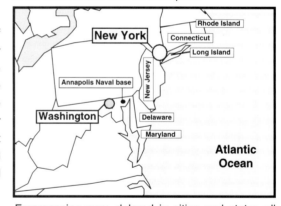

Emergencies were delared in cities and states all along the east coast. Schools were closed in New Jersey, Delaware, Maryland, New York, Rhode Island, and courts and other government offices were also shut. In these states emergency headquarters were set up to co-ordinate emergency and rescue services.

On Fire Island, off the coast of New York state, many residents evacuated to the mainland to stay in hotels or with relatives. Some however stayed on. They boarded up their windows and sat out the storm in their basements. Earlier there was panic buying at the shops, when locals stocked up on tins and dry goods.

Read through the newspaper article. This tells you about Hurricane Gloria which hit the United States.

Classification
Exemplar 2:
The response to Hurricane Gloria, USA

Task 1: Look at the headings given below. (i) Shade the 'action taken by authorities' heading in **red**. (ii) Shade the 'action taken by businesses' heading in **blue**. (iii) Shade the 'action taken by individuals' heading in **green**.

Task 2: Reread the article. (i) Using **red**, underline anything about action taken by **authorities**. (ii) Using **blue**, underline anything about action taken by **businesses**. (iii) Using **green**, underline anything about action taken by **individuals**.

Task 3: Use the information that you have underlined to write what you can into the correct boxes below.

Task 4: On a piece of lined paper, **describe** the different ways humans can respond to hurricanes and **give reasons** for these ways. Which do you think are the most effective in saving lives?

Try to suggest **other** measures we could take to help limit the damage of any future hurricanes.

RED — *Action taken by authorities*

BLUE — *Action taken by businesses*

GREEN — *Action taken by individuals*

Classification Exemplar 3: Changing iron & steel location

Context

This *Classification* activity was trialled with a number of different classes from Y9 to 11. All the work was taught as part of a unit of work on industry in two schools. These groups covered a wide range of ability. This was a deliberate attempt to demonstrate how this strategy can be differentiated. Previous material covered by the groups included: employment structure, and factors affecting the location of primary, secondary and tertiary industry.

With the younger groups the intention was to develop a robust framework for thinking about industrial location. With older groups doing GCSE, it provided an example of changing industrial location.

Preparation

Two alternative approaches to the task are presented here, therefore you need to decide which approach is more appropriate to the class you are teaching. You might also like to develop a hybrid version.

The more structured version is easier to do and the outcomes are more predictable and reliable. The more open version is harder for pupils to do; it is therefore riskier, but the outcomes are potentially more powerful. You should not however assume that the more open version is a non-starter for lower ability classes. If a class is positive with reasonable self esteem, they may be able to tackle the open version.

The simpler version comprises a number of small, achievable tasks on CLASSIFICATION RESOURCE SHEET 6. For the open version you need to cut up the statements on CLASSIFICATION RESOURCE SHEET 7 and put them in envelopes, one envelope per pair.

Launching

This is another opportunity to use the introductory *Classification* exercise (CLASSIFICATION RESOURCE SHEET 1, and instructions on page 116). This is very powerful. If classes have done *Classification* tasks before they may not need too much invitation to get into the task. One further way in is to read a simple passage to the pupils. However, before you do this you should give some simple instructions:

> 'As I read, put your left hand up if I mention a place, and put up your right hand if I mention a person.'

If you can find nothing better to read you can use the following:

> 'Michael Fish (**right** hand) *is famous for his weather forecast when he said that a hurricane would not be striking Southern England* (**left**) *that night. Luckily the north* (**left**) *did not suffer too badly. However in counties like Sussex and Kent* (**left**) *huge areas of woodland were virtually destroyed. One elderly lady* (**right**) *at Seal in Kent* (**left**) *said that it looked as though Gulliver* (**right**) *had stamped through the woods, called the Chart* (**left**).'

Instructions

This section is split into two: the simple version and the open version.

The simple version

1. Produce an OHT of CLASSIFICATION RESOURCE SHEET 6 and read the reports **A** and **B** to the class.

2. Refer back to Michael Fish. In that case, the pupils were listening and classifying as they went along: people and places. If you have used the newspaper adverts exercise, you can refer back to that as well. Make the point that if you have good categories in your head when you read or listen to something you can make better sense of it—it is like having a

---

This exemplar demonstrates an interesting relationship. As the degree of openness of an activity increases, so does the risk, but so does the possible learning.

This is a powerful bridging activity and establishes a broader purpose for the task.

This is metacognition again.

> **Classification Exemplar 3: Changing iron & steel location**

fishing net instead of your fingers when you are rock-pooling, you can scoop up or catch the things in the water much better. Reading or listening without some categories in your head implies that most of the meaning and information will 'slip through your fingers'.

3. Go through a worked example, referring to the OHT.
4. Give a 20 minute time-limit either to underline or classify the information into the boxes.
5. After 20 minutes ask for feedback on what they have done.
6. Explain the extended writing task, and talk them through the writing framework, for example *'The iron and steel works moved from the valley to the ports because....'.*

The open version

1. Start with the second instruction above about Michael Fish.
2. Give out the envelopes containing the statements on CLASSIFICATION RESOURCE SHEET 7 to pairs and tell pupils to take the pieces of paper out. Explain that about half the pieces relate to South Wales in the nineteenth century, and about half to the present. They need to do two things: firstly, sort the pieces into the two time-periods, and then into locational factors. The locational factors for the two time-periods should overlap but should not be identical.

Managing the activity

For lower ability groups (whether doing the simpler or more open version) it is important to support their reading of the text. We often underestimate pupils' ability on the basis of their reading—the two do not always correlate. Apart from help that you give, you can also sit better readers next to less able ones.

Otherwise the most important issue is to maintain the pupils' commitment, either by praising good decisions and work, or by gently raising doubts with them over their classification. As ever, if they are doing well, don't interfere too much, but listen instead.

In the case of the open version, there are two things that you might be called on to do: firstly, point out inconsistencies in their time grouping, such as *'Can both those apply to the same time period?'* Secondly, you can help by giving names to the factors that pupils identify.

Debriefing

This has varied with classes. It is generally important to keep using the word **classifying** so that it becomes part of their vocabulary. With lower ability groups much of the debriefing has taken place whilst they have been working on the activity using questions such as:

'Where do you think that we have done classifying before?'

'Does putting things into groups help you organise things in other subjects or even at home?'

'Are there important categories or groupings used in other subjects?'

'Can you think of shops that use classifying as a way of organising where they put things in the shop?'

> *This is an interesting variation on debriefing—done with individuals and pairs rather than with the whole class. The down side will be that the best thinking in the class has not been accessed.*

The reaction to these questions is mixed—there are blank looks— but the shop question usually works with almost everyone (supermarkets, music stores, department stores, shoe shops, etc). Many pupils remember the adverts task and some are able clearly to see the importance of groupings in other subjects, such as ingredients in food technology. Raising this awareness is a slow process, but it feels valuable. It is a shame that it is so foreign to them.

**Classification
Exemplar 3:
Changing iron &
steel location**

This is bridging (see page 162).

Metacognition being developed (see page 159).

This demonstrates the real power of pupils developing a rich vocabulary for the subject—the secret garden of the curriculum becomes less secret!

For the more open version, a higher order debrief can be tackled. There are a great many issues that can be opened up. To make a start we suggest three questions:

1. *'Once you had put the information into the time groups what did you have to do?'* This gets straightforward answers: they had to decide on locational factors. You can explain here that there were two stages in the classification: by time and then by factor. Be deliberate about the use of the word factor—a heading that can be seen to be important in decision making or changes. You can make the point that classifying can be in stages, breaking information down into smaller and smaller groups. You might be able to make a link with animal classification in science.

2. *'What happened to your listening during the Michael Fish story and why?'* They make the point that they listened hard for the people and places because they were listening for it. Make the point that they can always listen out hard for things if they prepare their brain with an 'advance organiser' (it is like having a better radio receiver, which is tuned in to the wavelength).

3. *'What happened when you were reading the "snippets"?'* They will tell you something to the effect that they were looking for information to link it to the time periods. You can make the link with the listening exercise. When you have categories in your mind it helps you look at and deal with text. Words like factors, cause, effect, advantage, disadvantage, changes and conflicts are central to classifying much of the information we bump into in geography.

Follow-up

For both approaches CLASSIFICATION RESOURCE SHEET 8 provides a framework for writing up the work. The top half helps to clarify the importance of the different factors and how they have changed. The pupils should do the outer two columns before tackling the middle one. Talking this through helps a lot with lower ability groups. For these, too, a small change to the lower box works wonders: give one more sentence start: *'Another reason the location changed was...'*. This really encourages them to go that little bit further in giving their understanding and therefore it is another form of differentiation. For many more able pupils the bottom frame does not give enough space and they should write in their books or on paper.

Read through the two extracts below. These tell you why the iron and steel industry changed location in South Wales.

Classification Exemplar 3:

Changing iron & steel location

Extract A: 100 years ago

South Wales has a large number of iron and steel producing factories. They make one third of the iron and steel in the country. To make steel you need good quality iron ore, coal and limestone. All of these raw materials are found locally and have been mined and quarried in the area for years.

The easiest places to mine the coal are the bottoms of the valleys, where it is also easiest to build factories on the flat land. The factories in the area provide work for thousands of people who have lived all their lives in the valley. They also employ many people who have come here to find work.

The valleys have provided many ways to power the steel industry. Rivers and coal have provided steam power for many years. The valleys are also good as they have good road, rail and canal links to nearby ports on the south coast. The steel is transported to these ports and is then shipped abroad. It is sold all over the world.

Extract B: In the 1990s?

South Wales now has only three iron and steelworks. It has the advantages of good, deep water ports to handle the cheap imports of iron ore and coal from abroad. Around these ports the major iron and steelworks have grown up in the available space left by older industries. They have found that by locating near to the point where these raw materials are unloaded, they save money by not having to transport them a long distance. Limestone is still quarried locally.

The iron and steel manufacturers in South Wales have also seen that by locating similar types of factories together, they can save money on production costs.

The steel industry that is located in this region has benefitted from government grants and low taxes, making the costs of running a large steelworks much cheaper than anywhere else in the country.

Electricity is used to power the steelworks. Few workers are needed, because of steelworks closing down and more machinery being used. Transporting the steel to the rest of the country is easy. There are good road and rail links. Nowadays, there is less need to ship the steel to the rest of the world. This is because there are other countries who produce steel cheaper and have a larger market to sell to.

Classification Exemplar 3: Changing iron & steel location

Why did the iron and steel industry change location?

Read through the two reports on page 129. This tells you why.

Task 1: Look at the questions in the boxes below. Neatly shade each heading a different colour. Using the same coloured pencil as the heading, underline the relevant information in both extracts on page 129.

Task 2: Write up the answers in the correct boxes.

Task 3: In detail, write **why** the industry changed location?

Special grants available from the government (incentives)	*The land the factory is built on (site)*
In the past? In the 1990s?	In the past? In the 1990s?
Transport links used and reasons why	*Where they sell the steel (market)*
In the past? In the 1990s?	In the past? In the 1990s?
Raw materials used and where they are from	*Amount of people employed (labour)*
In the past? In the 1990s?	In the past? In the 1990s?
Power supply used for the steelworks	*Any other benefits of the location?*
In the past? In the 1990s?	In the past? In the 1990s?

Thinking Through Geography

Classification Resource Sheet 6

Statements—Locational factors

Classification Exemplar 3: Changing iron & steel location

1.	The valleys have good road, rail and canal links to nearby ports.
2.	The easiest place to build the factories was in the valley bottoms, where the land is flat and the coal is mined.
3.	Electricity is used to power the steelworks.
4.	Transporting the steel to the rest of the country is easy because there are good road and rail links.
5.	The factories are located near the port because this is where the raw materials are unloaded. This saves money because the raw materials do not have to be transported far.
6.	The steel is transported to the ports and is then shipped abroad and sold all over the world.
7.	To make steel you need good quality iron ore, coal and limestone. All of these are found locally and have been mined and quarried in the area for years.
8.	The valleys have provided power for the factories—coal is used in large quantities.
9.	Limestone is still quarried locally.
10.	The steelworks near the ports have benefited from government grants and low taxes.
11.	The remaining steelworks are located on the land left by old industries, which have now closed.

Continued...

Classification

Exemplar 3:

Changing iron & steel location

Statements continued...

12.	Fewer workers are needed because more machinery is used.
13.	South Wales has a large number of iron and steelworks.
14.	South Wales now has only three steelworks. It has the advantages of good, deep water ports to handle the cheap imports of iron ore and steel from abroad.
15.	By locating near the coast the manufacturers can be near other modern factories.
16.	The factories in the area provide work for thousands of people who have lived all their lives in the valley. They also employ many workers from other areas.
17.	Less of the steel is shipped abroad because many other countries produce cheaper steel.
18.	The factories make one third of the iron and steel in Britain.

Locational factors

Classification Exemplar 3: Changing iron & steel location

Task 1: How have the changes in the location factors of the iron and steel industry affected its position in South Wales?

Factors important in 1820	*How have these factors changed?*	*Factors important in 1990*

Task 2: In the space below you are going to complete the explanation of the changes in the location of the iron and steel industry. In your answer you should mention how some factors of location have remained important but changed their location, like raw materials. Also those which have changed in importance, either becoming more important like government grants, or less important, like the need to locate where there is labour to work.

Location of iron and steel production in South Wales has changed because...

Classification: Adapting the strategy

Essentially there are two main levels of activity here.

The first is where categories are given for pupils to use. This is fairly familiar to geography teachers. The added value, however, lies in making the categories visible and permanent in the heads of pupils so that they can anticipate their application in other contexts. If you read elsewhere in the book, you will notice that classifying underpins so many of the tasks such as **Fact or Opinion, Mysteries** and **Odd One Out**. There is mutual reinforcement in this.

> *Accessing 'best' thinking is one of the strongest justifications of collaborative learning and debriefing.*

The second category is more challenging where pupils have to develop categories for themselves. The danger is that their categories may be weak, but usually the debriefing process allows the best thinking to surface. The up side is that if pupils have derived and tested the categories themselves they are so much stronger and valid. The way to develop this is to find pieces of text that might usually be the basis of comprehension exercises. Then you chop up the text into boxes. This can be observed in the two variations of the iron and steel exercise.

Afterthoughts

All these activities have proved to be very successful when trialled in the classroom and they have seemed to be most effective when used as an integral or summative exercise in a unit of work. We can see a cumulative effect on classes who have done **Classification** activities two or three times. They are developing a vocabulary related to the concept and they are more confident in dealing with data. With the sort of writing structures demonstrated in this Chapter to guide them, they are also improving their writing. This is exciting.

However, there is a dilemma in using open **Classification** activities. To what extent do you allow pupils to develop their own categories through handling information, and to what extent do you provide them. There is almost certainly greater value in getting pupils to generate their own categories, because they are natural and meaningful. However, the down side is that their categories may not have maximum utility. With the exemplars in this section you can use either approach.

We would summarise the benefits as follows:
- the open-ended nature of the activities allows pupils to respond at their own level;
- pupils are able to talk about their ideas and attempt to justify their decisions;
- pupils of all abilities are highly motivated and enjoy these activities;
- pupil understanding is enhanced by these activities;
- peer relationships and group work are improved.

Colleagues may be initially wary of the technique, but their confidence will grow if they are provided with clear guidance. It may be an idea to trial the activity in a departmental INSET session to help everyone see the potential benefits, and to get a feel of the shape and purpose of the activity.

Reading Photographs

Rationale

Textbooks are full of photographs. A typical KS3 textbook has between 2 and 4 on most double-pages and there are a great many more diagrams in addition. Yet rarely in textbooks are photographs used for more than general illustration, and sometimes their only function seems to be to break up the text and introduce colour. However the photopacks from charities and Development Education Centres do show that photographs can be used as a major resource around which to structure challenging learning activities.

There can be little doubt that visual literacy, in the broadest sense, is required in the late-twentieth century and for the new millennium. We live in a highly visual society, saturated with television, cinema, billboard and magazine images and we owe it to pupils to help them decode the information in those media. And, at a much more practical level, there are real advantages in being able to read photographs in the pursuit of higher achievement. GCSE and A Level examination papers use photographs and sketches extensively and many pupils miss marks by not using the information that is readily available within them. Further still, the increasing trend towards decision making papers in examinations demands a capability in using visual images.

Thinking Through Geography activities generally seek to develop pupils' abilities to use all their senses (see page 162).

However, we give little explicit attention to the skills embedded in the process. As with so much in education we expect it to happen by osmosis—it permeates the curriculum, which usually means that it does not happen at all. There is an explicit reference to photographs in the Statutory Orders for geography. At KS3, para 3g states that *'pupils should be taught to select and use secondary sources of evidence—photographs (including vertical and oblique aerial photographs), satellite images, and other sources... to inform their studies'*. It is a rather limp injunction, but it is there!

Explicit attention to decoding skills is encouraged by metacognition.

At present we see three rich seams to exploit in photographs. Firstly, and very obviously, we want to get pupils to look more carefully at photographs to see more of what is there; to scan rather than skim. Secondly, we want to get pupils to go beyond what they can see and make connections between what is visible and what they already know. Finally, we want them to start speculating and hypothesising using the evidence in the photograph. This would imply questions such as: *'What happened prior to the instant of the click of the shutter?' 'What happened after?' 'Why were those people there and how did this place come to be like this anyway?'* This is the essence of the enquiry process. The exemplars included in this section are designed to encourage pupils to develop their ability to do all three.

*Making connections would be part of the process of **constructing** personal meaning from the photograph.*

It should be recognised also that the use of photographs is a major vehicle in differentiation. Pupils do not need to be able to read text, and therefore in many ways using photos removes some of the barriers to information that text imposes. By using photographs you can begin to unlock some of the unused talent in low-achieving pupils and, in the process, boost their self-esteem.

Reading Photographs

Exemplar 1:

Using photos to introduce geography

This rationale is a neat paraphrase of Thinking Through Geography activities.

Creating a good talk environment is a prerequisite for developing metacognition and collaborative learning (see page 160).

Context

This exercise was designed initially as an introductory activity for geography at the start of Y7, with a mixed ability class, to avoid nose-diving into map skills. It serves the purposes of:

- introducing a wide range of issues and themes to be studied at KS3;
- raising awareness of the importance of cognitive skills in geography (I want them to recognise from their first week in our school that doing geography is not just about learning facts, it is equally about learning to learn);
- showing the inherent inter-relatedness of the themes and issues in the subject;
- demonstrating that it is a brilliant and enjoyable subject;
- getting pupils used to the idea that they will learn a great deal by listening to each other in small groups and in the whole class.

One of the advantages of having mixed ability groups is that pupils can learn from each other, but this can only happen if there is quality talk between pupils in both small and large groups. I try to build an atmosphere in which pupils can talk comfortably and (critically) not be afraid of being wrong. I want them to learn over time that sharing your first thoughts with others is a healthy way of developing and refining ideas—a sort of redrafting of ideas through talk. This activity is an important first step down that road.

To demonstrate the flexibility of the resource, I have used the very same activity with Y9 and Y11 during revision.

Preparation

The primary resource is the set of black and white photos (READING PHOTOGRAPHS RESOURCE SHEET 1) that can be photocopied. (Modern photocopiers do a pretty good job once you get the buttons set correctly.) Once copied and cut up, the photos need to be labelled with a letter or number for reference. My photocopies have now been mounted on card, laminated and finished off with a sticky label with a number on in the corner. The number helps tremendously in whole class instructions or discussions.

If you wish to try the type of launching I developed (see below) you will need some holiday snaps, preferably your own.

Pupils will work first in pairs, but later in 4s so it may be advisable to give some thought to how to construct the 4s in the classroom, although this was not a problem with this class, who were eager and malleable.

Assuming that you use any or all of the photographs on RESOURCE SHEET 1 you will need to know where and what they are.

Photograph 1	Cassava factory, Java, Indonesia.
Photograph 2	Cooling towers in Yorkshire taken from the A1, England.
Photograph 3	Fold mountains, Sisteron, France.
Photograph 4	Eldon Square Shopping Centre, Newcastle City Centre, England
Photograph 5	Paddy fields, Bali, Indonesia.
Photograph 6	Disused warehouses, Newcastle's quayside, England.
Photograph 7	'Ladies in Hats'—stone capped pillars produced by erosion, Embrun, France.
Photograph 8	Anthracite mine, near Lyon, France.

Photograph 9	Cement factory, Gateshead, England.
Photograph 10	Fosse Park Shopping Centre, Leicester, England.
Photograph 11	Central Gateshead, England.
Photograph 12	Farm near Mickletrafford, Chester, England.

Reading Photographs Exemplar 1: Using photos to introduce geography

Some possible combinations are as follows (but remember that they are not the only answers):

1 and 5	Growing and processing a food crop;
1 and 6	Factories;
1 and 12	Agriculture or growing crops;
2 and 8	Coal is burned in power stations;
3 and 7	Rocks, weathering or erosion;
4 and 10	Shops.

Launching

You cannot assume that a Y7 pupil will understand you if you say **Reading Photographs**. My way in was to hold up a holiday photo album and pose the question: *'If you had to tell someone about my holiday without talking to me about where I had been or what I had done, what would you look for in the photos to help you?'* This really hooked them, but it does take up valuable time and could be dispensed with if used with older classes.

I walked up and down the rows with the album giving them a quick look and turning a few pages (avoiding any sensitive ones!). They were craning their necks and leaning out of their seats. They were able to spot the sort of things I had done on holiday (in Peru) fairly easily, which included walking, visiting ancient ruins, waiting at airports, shopping in local markets and a small amount of sitting around eating and drinking! But as to where I had been, they were struggling—they had to look at the weather and vegetation, the clothes that the local people were wearing, whether the water was a lake or the sea, the architecture of the contemporary buildings and the ruins, any signs or writing to indicate the language or place names.

Through question and answer I developed a simple model on the board of what they had done:

- searched for evidence in the photo;
- formed an initial theory or deduction based on the evidence;
- looked for confirming or conflicting evidence by looking at several photos, ie, cross-checking;
- drawn a firm(ish) conclusion.

The task is scaffolded carefully, and structured carefully.

The explicit elaboration of what steps have been undertaken is part of the process of developing metacognition (see page 159).

I wanted pupils to see that they had done more than make a wild guess and that the process involved had stages—looking, coming up with ideas (theorising), checking, comparing, and reasoning. Over time I expect this process to become embedded in their approach to problem solving.

This took about 10 minutes. It could have taken a great deal longer, as there was a great deal to talk about, but I felt that there was a limit to the amount of discussion that some members of the class could tolerate.

Although I did not do this in the trial, I have considered a very brief pairing activity as a bridge into the first activity. It requires 6 items drawn on an OHT: a car, a horse, a daffodil, a cart, a tree, and a lorry, each with an identifying letter. Ask everyone to put these 6 items into 3 pairs and to jot down the pairs of letters. Most will put the daffodil and tree together as plants. But the horse may be put with the cart or the

Reading Photographs

Exemplar 1: Using photos to introduce geography

car. You may make the point that there are a variety of links possible. I have not found this necessary with mixed ability classes but it could be helpful with a low-achieving class as an extra step.

Instructions

1. I distributed the sets of photos to the pupil pairs and told them to pair up all the photos by making connections between them. (Do remind them that this is not like Pellmanism—there are a host of possible and acceptable pairings, although some may be better than others.) You might need to do one with them to give them confidence, eg, photos 4 and 10 both show shops. Ask them to do this seriously. (There is a real problem here about not being too heavy and suppressing creative thinking but at the same time discouraging the smartalecs who might link 2 photos by saying that one has someone who looks like their cousin Louise, and another has someone who looks like their cousin Sam—this is where your skill comes in.) I told the class that they could only write down the numbers when they had paired all the photos.

2. Having written down the paired numbers, they were told to write a brief explanation of the connection between them. Both pupils need to do this. Ideally they should use a geographical term gathered from general knowledge or their KS2 course. This class had no great problem here. Alternatively, you could provide a list of terms that they could use, but at present I feel that this might steer their choices and thinking too much, as they might look for right answers. (This is another place where your professional skill comes in.)

3. Once this was done, pairs had to join up to make 4s to compare their results. Give them a time allocation of between 5 and 10 minutes to do this. Tell them not to argue about who has got the best pairings. Tell them to take it in turn to explain one of their links. The other pair must listen and look for what they think are good links to do with geography. The aim therefore is to pick up good ideas from the other pair. Tell them that you will be asking pairs to explain the links *made by the other pair* and not their own, and therefore they need to listen hard for what they think is the best link. This part relates back strongly to my intention to train them to listen to each other and to share ideas.

Good thinking is being shared through this collaboration.

Managing the activity

With this Y7 class, management of behaviour was not a problem. They were very motivated and interested. My main role was reassurance and encouragement. However, I have learned a number of important lessons:

- It is very tempting to suggest connections between photos. Don't do this because they then think that there is a right answer. If they ask you, *'Is this OK?'*, just say, *'Well, what is your connection?'* As long as they say something fairly logical accept it. It is process, not product, that you are seeking. However, if you really think that the reasoning is weak, I would go as far as saying, *'Could you connect those two?'*, indicating one of the pair and another unpaired photo.

This reticence helps to maintain ambiguity

- They tend to do the first few fairly easily because some things jump out. It gets harder as the number of photos reduces and the number of possible links reduces. This is when the most creative thinking is required or when the daft stuff creeps in. Some pairs can be encouraged to reassess some earlier pairs, whereas some get very down at this suggestion. Be prepared to accept some floppy links towards the end like, *'These two both have sky in!'*

This is part of a process of encouraging checking and refining.

- As with most other activities in the book, try listening a while to what they are saying. It can be very revealing and very different from what gets said in whole class discussion. If you overhear good thinking, you can ask the pair to share it with the class later.
- Don't wait for the last pair to finish. Give time warnings like, *'I'm only going to give you another 2 minutes'*.
- Some pairs are very quick, but not necessarily thoughtful. You can ask them either to look for, and record, alternative pairings or to find differences between their pairs of photos.
- You may have planned pairs and 4s, but either the number in the class or absences may destroy your arithmetic, so just use your initiative.
- When the pairs are put together to make 4s, monitor that they are keeping to your instruction and that they are not arguing—if necessary repeat that their job is to find out what the other pair came up with.

Reading Photographs Exemplar 1: Using photos to introduce geography

Differentiation by task.

Debriefing

Remember that this was the first lesson for a Y7 class and the main objective was to begin to establish some ground rules and expectations for the year. The intention therefore was to get them to talk and to listen carefully. This was achieved for the most part and, with some prompting, various individuals volunteered their connections and the explanation for them. The main difficulty was that they were too timid to challenge one another or even extend an explanation. Once one answer had been given for a connection between one photo and any other, it was difficult to elicit another connection between the first one and a new (different) photo. Perhaps one should not expect too much too quickly—at least they did listen. The high point was a passage that went roughly as follows:

Me: *'What makes the best connection?'*

Pupil 1: *'The one with the best explanation.'*

Me: *'What makes a good explanation?'*

Pupil 2: *'Where you use what you see in the picture.'*

Pupil 3: *'When the other person understands what you are telling them.'*

With probing, it was possible to get them to say a great deal about what they could see in the photographs, although they still tended to go for the more obvious connections. Perhaps I had said too much to expect them to be divergent.

The Flowchart (READING PHOTOGRAPHS RESOURCE SHEET 2) gives you a model to work from in your debriefing.

140

Reading Photographs

Exemplar 1:

Using photos to introduce geography

❶

❷

❸

❹

Reading Photographs
Exemplar 1:
Using photos to introduce geography

⑤

⑥

⑦

⑧

Reading Photographs Resource Sheet 1

Thinking Through Geography

Reading Photographs

Exemplar 1: Using photos to introduce geography

Flowchart for debriefing—making connections

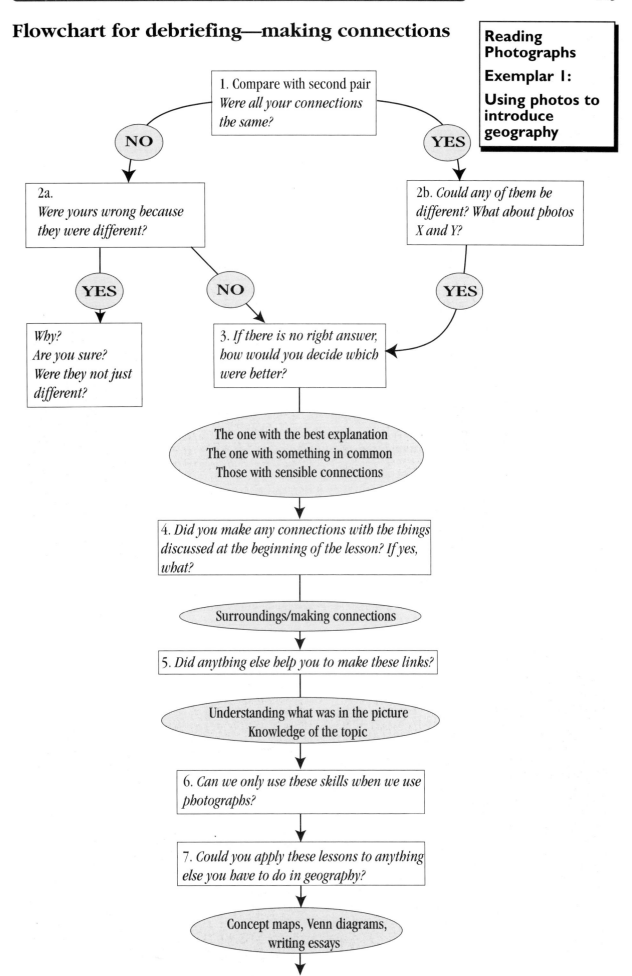

Reading Photographs

Exemplar 2:

Urban land use models

The unlocking of students' knowledge is a major theme in this book.

Context

This activity was trialled with three Y11 groups, but the write-up concentrates on the low ability group, which comprised just 12 boys (it is a mixed sex school). They were very disruptive.

The class had recently undertaken GCSE coursework, which focused on the hypothesis that residential quality improves with distance from the CBD, which was grounded in the Burgess concentric zones model. In previous years the low achieving students had not done well in drawing conclusions and had therefore sacrificed too many marks. One of the problems that they seemed to have was putting the housing that they recorded into the context of the area in which it was found, ie, they tended to see residential quality merely in terms of the structural quality of the housing, taking no notice of the local environment. This was especially the case in their discussion. The decision to use this photograph exercise was an attempt to unlock the students' knowledge of urban areas.

Part of the problem with teaching land use models is that, because they are so generalised and do not provide a good fit to actual cities, students find it hard to relate their local city/large town to the model and vice-versa. By using photos they can relate the more intimate, visible features of urban landscapes, as they know them, to the models and, in the process, question the model.

Although this activity related to the Burgess model, it is worth pointing out that the Burgess model need play no part in the activity, especially as it seems to be slipping out of most GCSE syllabuses. Instead one can simply refer to inner city, pre-war suburbs, post-war suburbs, council estates, private estates or whatever nomenclature fits your context best.

Preparation

Reproduce the photographs. I like to preserve the good copies, once I have them, either in plastic wallets or by lamination. I stuck the photos to the wall in the classroom, so that the students could wander round and look at them. It is my experience that nearly all classes, but especially low ability groups, behave well when they are invited to wander round the room, as they were to do here. Sitting still for a long period is not a natural state for many. I also located enough clipboards, (one for each student); this also appeals and keeps their hands occupied.

This signals a changed relationship and expectation.

Launching

I started by putting up an OHT of the Burgess model. I reminded them what and where the zones were. I asked them where St James's Park (Newcastle United's ground) would be on the model. They answered this in two stages. Firstly, they said that the ground was near the city centre and, secondly, from there they were able to tell me that it was in the Zone in Transition. I then said that many football grounds were in similar locations. (Sadly, because these students have very little experience of anything in Britain outside Tyneside, they could not respond.) I then pointed to the photographs on the walls and said *'In which photo are you most likely to find a league football ground?'* They were fairly split—choosing either 2 or 3—but in the process they had started to look carefully at the photos and to speculate on what part of a city they would be in.

Instructions

I gave out READING PHOTOGRAPHS RESOURCE SHEETS 3 and 4 and asked the students to consider each statement in turn and match it to a photo. We did the first one together. Again they were a bit puzzled, so I had to water it down slightly and say, *'Where do most buses start from in the city?'* or *'Where do you find most big shops?'*

They could answer this and from there it was a small step for them to identify the CBD in Photograph 1 as the most likely location.

It was fairly easy from here to communicate the idea that they had to work their way through each statement and write down a few words for their reasons for allocating a statement to a photo.

Managing the activity

I am always a bit surprised when I take risks with a tricky group and it works, and this was no exception. The clipboard helps; maybe they just feel different. I moved around the photos and talked to individuals in a whisper. Oddly, they copied this behaviour and only whispered to each other (which was bizarre) as I expected them to be boisterous. I pointed a few things out to them and again (unusually) they helped each other. None of the statements caused insurmountable problems: the most difficult turned out to be the one about derelict buildings. The asthma statement gave a chance for the chronic asthma sufferer to shine. They tried to shock me by saying that you could buy drugs anywhere, and did I want any? There is no doubt that they enjoyed the lesson and it really got them thinking. It helped that they did not have to read or write much, and I kept nagging them to record their answers.

Follow-up

The follow-up was the coursework, where the results were incorporated into their conclusions. It is impossible to say whether this activity resulted in the students gaining more marks overall, but they seemed to have more awareness of the actual character of urban areas, not because they had been taught, but because they started to use their own knowledge.

Debriefing

We talked a little about exams—the exam papers have photographs which contain lots of information which can be used. I also encouraged them to think in the exam about what they knew from their own experience. In truth, I don't think that this had too much impact, because it came too late for this group; Y7 is the place to start (see the previous exemplar).

Reading Photographs

Exemplar 2:

Urban land use models

The whole of this process encourages students to use their own knowledge which was a prime purpose of the activity (see page 157).

Reading Photographs

Exemplar 2: Urban land use models

1 Eldon Square, Newcastle. CBD.

2 Byker Wall. Inner city redevelopment Zone in transition

3 Gateshead. Low class residential

Continued...

Reading Photographs Exemplar 2: Urban land use models

4 Jesmond, Newcastle. Medium class residential.

5 1950s Council estate, Gateshead

6 Mickletrafford, Chester. High class residential.

Reading Photographs

Exemplar 2:

Urban land use models

In which photo are you most likely to...

1. ... be able to catch a bus to visit friends anywhere in the city?

2. ... get your car stolen?

3. ... be in a bad place for asthma sufferers to live?

4. ... see a fox at night?

5. ... get chewing gum stuck on your shoe?

6. ... upset someone by parking outside their house?

7. ... see steeplejacks working?

8. ... have derelict buildings?

9. ... have people complaining about noise from their neighbours?

10. ... be able to get milk at 10.30. at night?

11. ... have schools with good examination results?

12. ... be able to buy drugs?

13. ... have a local garden centre?

Context

This activity was designed for use with a Y12 A Level group. There were 18 in the group (13 males and 5 females). There was a considerable spread of ability and, in comparison to some groups, they were generally forthcoming and willing to discuss their ideas openly. The syllabus concerned was the London (ULEAC) Syllabus B—Module B Theme 3 *Living and Leisure*. The group had recently finished studying 'Population and Settlement' and in this section on leisure and tourism had studied National Parks generally and looked at two case studies in particular: (i) St Lucia and (ii) the Masai Mara in Kenya. In both cases there had been some emphasis on efforts to protect the resource base at the heart of the industry, and the impact of the industry on the local inhabitants and culture. Soon after this lesson they were due to embark on some individual research on three tourism case studies. Having said all this, I feel that the outcomes were so valuable and generic that the activity (unchanged) would pay for itself at any time in Y12.

This example goes a step further than the first two exemplars in this Chapter and requires greater powers of deduction based on evidence. Therefore it is tapping the third seam in the rationale, and higher level skills are required.

Preparation

Logistics were slightly less of a problem than in the other exemplars. I needed to encourage a framework of thinking that went beyond what was in the picture and beyond the confines of the lens; *'What was in the mind of the photographer?'* *'What might have been in the minds of the people being photographed?'*, and therefore, *'What might have been the impact of the photograph?'* I wanted students to consider whether photographs are neutral, just capturing what was in the way, or whether they have an agenda: *'Whether they composed in any way to make an argument or to represent a point of view?'* We do this with text on occasions and I felt that A Level students should begin to do it for visual images.

As I had bigger copies of the photos than are reproduced in this book I decided to hang them round the room. (I cleared some space and pinned them up before the lesson.) This allows the students to wander around the room and critically, I think, reinforces the notion that enquiry and exploration are active processes. Students have to be active and go to the resource, rather than sit passively waiting for the resource. During the lesson I felt that this was a crucial ingredient of the success of the activity.

Launching

I started with the Euro '96 England football matches, which were on at the time. I said that English newspapers had photos the next day of the English players after the famous penalty miss—pictures of despair and gloom. The German newspapers on the other hand had pictures of the German players celebrating. I pointed out that the English players were looking at the ground or had their heads in their hands, while the German players had their heads up and were acknowledging the German crowd and media. I asked why the two sets of newspapers had such fundamentally different photographs. (Actually some English newspapers had both types.)

This worked better than I had expected (although I had to stop the boys going on too much about the football and watch that some of the girls did not get bored). The discussion delivered many interesting starting points: photographs are taken for a reason (usually: the camera is deliberately pointed to get a particular image to match the reason; the people in the photo react to the camera, perhaps turning away, perhaps celebrating). The students were ready.

A bridging activity (see page 162).

Reading Photographs

Exemplar 3:

The impact of tourism (A Level)

Instructions

The recording sheet (READING PHOTOGRAPHS RESOURCE SHEET 6) takes the place of much specific instruction. But having given out the sheet I made the following observations:

1. *'The photos are mine. I am a geography teacher and I don't like package tours. I like to have a cultural experience on holiday, but even doing that you have an effect and invade privacy.'* (You could put this in the third person: *'These photographs were taken by a geography teacher who…'*.)

2. Ask students to move around the room in no particular order and complete the sheet, making sure to record the number of the photo and its location. Most particularly, they should think about why I [she] had gone to this place and taken the photo.

Managing the activity

This observation is a hallmark of the Thinking Through Geography approach.

In this situation I was definitely managing the activity and not the class, by which I mean that I felt I was concentrating on managing and facilitating the students' learning rather than managing their motivation or behaviour (a good feeling to have from time to time). They said things like, *'Oh look at that'*, or *'What about that?'* They asked questions about places and shouted questions, prompts or suggestions across the room to each other. They were genuinely enquiring of me and of each other. They were surprised that I had been to these places, and stunned (it seemed) at the idea that people actually applied geographical ideas to real places that they visit. One seemed astonished that I went trekking, as he has a particular interest in outdoor pursuits.

Debriefing

The recording sheet was the focus of the debriefing. I concentrated on asking why the photographs had been taken and what might be the impact. Of course because they were my photographs there were a number of diversions, but I was amazed at their interpretations of my motives. Sometimes they were spot on, as with the Cuzco photo, but at other times they were miles away. More importantly, they had clearly looked at the photographs very carefully, paying attention both to the detail and to the composition.

Reading Photographs

Exemplar 3:

The impact of tourism (A Level)

Continued...

Reading Photographs

Exemplar 3:

The impact of tourism (A Level)

Continued...

Texts for photographs

Reading Photographs Exemplar 3: The impact of tourism (A Level)

A **Machu Pichu, Peru.** *'This is undoubtedly the best known and most spectacular site on the continent. During the busy, dry season months of June to September up to 1,000 people a day come to visit the "lost city of the Incas", as Machu Pichu is popularly known. Despite the huge tourist influx, the site manages to retain its air of grandeur and mystery and remains a must for all visitors.'* (Lonely Planet: Peru.)

Although it is possible to drive, it is more common to take the train from Cuzco to Aguas Calientes then take the tourist bus up to the ruins. The more adventurous can trek for three days along the spectacular Inca Trail, although beware of altitude sickness! The best views are obtained if you trek in early, and watch the sun come up over the ruins, long before the hundreds of other tourists arrive. The rather tacky gift stalls, which seem to come with the territory, and the price of the bottled water, take the gloss off the almost religious splendour of the site.

B **The Uros Islands, Lake Titicaca, Peru.** The people of Uros live on floating reed islands, which have become a major tourist attraction and sadly over commercialised (evident from the number of boats in the picture and the litter spread around the islands). About 300 people still live on the islands and in the words of the tourist guides the lives of the people are interwoven with the reeds which grow in the shallows of Lake Titicaca. The reeds are used to make the islands themselves, which are built up in layers. As the reeds rot from the bottom more are added to the top. You have to watch that you don't put your foot through a rotten section!

C **Cuzco, Peru.** Cuzco is a beautiful city, 3,326 m above sea level. The photo shows two local cholla women and their llama. The women would not normally be in their best dresses, but they do so to earn a few coins from tourists who want photographs of 'traditional' life. It was also the cleanest llama I saw in 6 weeks. The irony is further demonstrated by the rubbish skip and the ever faithful Coca-Cola machine found even in the remotest parts of the world.

D **Jungle trip, near Trinidad, Eastern Bolivia (not the West Indies).** The photo was taken on a three-day trip up a tributary of the river Amazon from Trinidad. The party comprised three tourists and two guides (seen in the photo). The woman is Bolivian, but educated in the US. We travelled in a fairly primitive dugout with an outboard engine, which intruded into the peace of the region. We camped in the tour company's red square tent in complete contrast to the three bamboo huts which housed three families who earned their living from fishing in the river. The area was rich in wildlife and vegetation through which we trekked during the day, collecting wood for a fire on which to cook the piranha we caught. This is small-scale tourism, yet undoubtedly has an impact on a simple society where poverty, bigamy, ill health and danger from wild animals are facts of life.

E **Cassava Factory, Pangandaran, Java, Indonesia.** This is a family business where men, women and children work in sweltering conditions processing cassava to make a large savoury 'cake' with the texture of a prawn cracker and dyed in every conceivable colour. Trooping in to watch the work was extremely interesting but very intrusive. Some seemed more pleased to see us than others, but I generally felt that we were hindering the hard work that continued from dawn to dusk. Children were invaluable in the process as they were the only ones small enough to sit under the makeshift machine pureeing the cassava into spirals which could then be left to rise and later deep fried to produce the final product. Although the work was hard, everyone lived in relative comfort, was well fed and three generations were gainfully employed. One could criticise the use of child labour, but it seems to fit in with the context of this quiet fishing town. The alternative may have been moving to Jakarta, eking a living selling newspapers, chewing gum or drinks in a very dangerous urban environment.

F **Pra Loup, Nr. Barcolonette, France.** A ski station, 1,600 m above sea level. The photo was taken on a geography field trip in May. This excursion was to study the erosion on the slopes created by intensive skiing in winter. You can see the chairlift if you look closely. The resort makes a great effort to attract tourists all year round by diversifying its activities—the area also boasts whitewater rafting, mountain biking and walking. Students should be encouraged to infer as much as they can about the area from what they can see.

Reading Photographs
Exemplar 3: The impact of tourism (A Level)

PHOTO NUMBER 1–6	LOCATION A–F	ATTRACTION OF THE TOURISM AREA	ADVANTAGES	DISADVANTAGES

Thinking Through Geography — Reading Photographs Resource Sheet 6

Reading Photographs: Adapting the strategy

To recap, the exemplars here encourage students to look more closely at photographs, to make connections with what they already know and to speculate around the purpose and composition of photographs. If you want to extend your use of this strategy, then you need to make a collection of photographs. Many teachers will be familiar with the idea of cutting stories out of the newspapers, often with a photograph, but we would go further and encourage you to cut out striking photographs, whether the story is relevant or not. However, this inevitably leads to taking your own photographs. This is clearly not something new, but instead of taking photographs just of typical examples of phenomena, you might like to consider taking sets to stimulate and raise questions.

We have made various suggestions for activities involving sets of photographs and all of these are easily adapted to other sets and topics. However we decided to finish by dropping in a few more ideas about using photographs:

- **Story-boarding.** Run off between 4 and 8 photos for each pair in a class. You have to make a good choice and give them some direction, but the task is to put the photographs in a sequence either to give an account of events or to explain something.

- **Making connections.** Each individual or pair gets a copy of a photograph, arranged so that there is blank space around the image. The task is to make a connection between anything that can be seen in the picture and anything that has been covered in earlier lessons in the topic or in other topics.

- **Unfreezing.** This is a technique used by drama teachers. People who are frozen in the image are unfrozen. Students are asked what the people might be feeling or saying to each other, or what they might do next. If you have the taste for it you can arrange students in the poses in the photograph and let them act it out.

> *Story-boarding develops an insight into linkage which is so necessary to good explanation.*

Afterthoughts

The more I use photos the more they establish themselves in my mind as a fantastic resource that needs the same attention we give to worksheets, ie, a storage and retrieval system. Furthermore, you need to develop a constant habit of collecting photographs. As you develop activities using photographs you become acutely aware of the inadequacies of certain shots and the need for others. This creates the desire to go out and get your own. This has really brought home to me both the inadequacy of relying on textbooks and the seeming lack of thought that is given to their place in textbooks. Are they really just used to break up the text?

One gets hobby-horses and at the moment photographs come into that category. I may therefore be prejudiced but I feel that there is a very strong case for developing visual literacy—to develop the art of seeing. Students spend a great deal of time analysing poetry, plays and novels, but many of them don't read much. Why not give equal attention to analysing images which they cannot avoid seeing and being influenced by. I get cross now when I hear people sneering at media studies. I have come to appreciate that students experience the physical world largely through their eyes, whereas geography mainly draws on the spoken word and written text.

It has created an interesting agenda for talking to other members of staff, notably drama teachers and art teachers. Don't be put off if they see it initially as yet another attempt by geographers to take over the world.

Finally, there is no doubt in my mind that working with photographs in challenging ways develops thinking skills. It may be hard to pin down in any one lesson just what has been developed but over time my classes have become relatively expert in using photographs.

Curriculum Development

This part of the book is written for those who wish to go further than just using the materials or adapting the strategies to other contexts (Levels 1 and 2—see page 2). If you want to start building thinking into the geography curriculum and perhaps into the whole curriculum (Levels 3 and 4), then read on.

The work of the ***Thinking Through Geography*** Group has been motivated by a number of factors:

- The National Curriculum has had the unfortunate effect of making teachers play safe and cover content. Some of what was good in geography teaching has been lost.
- Many of the textbooks that have become popular as a result are too formulaic and undemanding. They cover the demands of the Programmes of Study but they rarely excite and motivate students.
- Many students leave school underachieving. Whilst a Grade D, E, F or G at GCSE may represent a great effort by a student and her/his teacher, it is a sad reflection on 11 years of compulsory school. Many able students do well at GCSE, but without becoming good learners, and they really struggle thereafter. We aim to see more students doing better.
- The example of Cognitive Acceleration, or Thinking Skills Programmes such as CASE (Cognitive Acceleration through Science Education), Instrumental Enrichment, Somerset Thinking Skills and Philosophy for Children. The evidence about the effects of these programmes on students' achievement and motivation encourages us to believe that we can teach more effectively (see Adey & Shayer, 1994).

We believe that there is a need for a reappraisal of the geography curriculum. Instead of trying to produce a curriculum that most students can cope with, there is a strong case for building a curriculum that changes the learner, so that they become effective learners and have access to a demanding curriculum. We do not pretend that this is easy. Furthermore, the strategies are aimed not only at less successful students, but are also highly suitable for the more able.

Curriculum design principles

It is hard to explain exactly how materials and strategies develop. It is partly a magical process that might be attributed to intuition or creative thinking. We can be clear, however, about some of the principles that have underpinned our approach to turning good ideas into successful materials and activities in the classroom. Some of these principles may appear a bit theoretical, but please persevere. Teaching tends to lack theoretical underpinning and the key to the really effective deployment of this approach lies in understanding and being able to use this theory.

1. Constructivism

In simple terms, **constructivism** implies that we learn through what we already know. When we say *'That makes no sense to me'*, we usually mean *'I have no mental resources to understand what I have seen or been told'*. If someone from Britain listens to a radio commentary on a tennis, football or cricket match, they will stand a good chance of understanding what is going on. If on the other hand they listen to a commentary on American football, hurling (Irish) or sumo wrestling most struggle to understand (despite the best efforts of Channel 4!). This is because few of us have much experience of these sports, so we do not have a mental framework through first-hand experience nor a language to interpret what is being said. It is not the fault of the commentator particularly: it is that we do not have an adequate receiver to interpret the words. So it is with students in many lessons: they do not have the mental frameworks to understand what is being delivered.

Many teachers already take account of this through their use of analogies, examples and stories. As a teacher, you use some knowledge that students already have to help them understand something new. Breathing on a window pane to demonstrate condensation is a very powerful medium to help students understand the atmospheric process. The much quoted teacher aphorism *'Start where the students are at'* is an expression of **constructivism**.

It is suggested that if new information can be interpreted through existing knowledge structures, termed **schema** (plural schemata) then it will be incorporated into a better understanding of a topic. If no connection can be made with existing knowledge then the new information will be lost—as 'water off a duck's back' (notice the use of analogy). It is hypothesised that there is a very productive and important mid-point between these conditions, where some connection is made but there is some mismatch between the incoming and the established knowledge. This is termed **cognitive conflict** and when and if resolved is associated with the formation of new concepts. Just occasionally we get a small window on this happening for a student, when they might say, with feeling, *'Ahh—I get it!'*

If one accepts the above then it should be understood that because everyone has somewhat different experiences and powers of perception then every individual constructs their own unique understanding of the world. If you do happen to have spent months training to be a sumo wrestler then you are better equipped to learn more about it.

So how does this idea of constructivism help in ***Thinking Through Geography***. It is incredibly hard and probably unrealistic to gauge the existing understanding of every student, so:

- On some occasions you can encourage students to access their existing knowledge and try to make it available for them to construct new understanding. ***Mind Movies*** and ***Living Graphs*** are obvious examples of this, but brain storming is another, especially where one is asking students what they already know.

- Provide experiences for students through which they understand a new topic or ideas. This may be through demonstrations, analogies, simulations, role plays, local fieldwork, practical homework tasks, etc. Such activities will often form part of the launching stage in a thinking lesson, such as the photo album as an introduction to ***Reading Photographs*** (see page 136); or the fruit used in the launching of the ***Odd One Out*** activity (see page 10).

- Give activities to students in which they can actively try new information against understanding they may already have. ***Mysteries*** are an example of this.

Finally in this section, brief mention is made of **situated cognition** (see Light & Butterworth, 1992). This view of learning emphasises the role of the group of learners sharing the act of learning to develop specialised knowledge and approaches to a particular context. In the introduction to this book, it was stressed that geography is a way of looking at the world. Through geographical education we need to be more explicit about the values, tools and practices of geography, so that students become geographers rather than people who know something about geography. It is important therefore that the contexts presented to students have some value and authenticity: they need to matter to them. **Launching** helps to do this and **bridging** at the end adds further relevance, but a crucial test of success is whether students take themselves seriously as learners.

For a short introduction to constructivism, the introductory Chapter of *Making Sense of Secondary Science* (Driver, Squires, Rushworth & Wood-Robinson, 1994) serves well, but for a more full but diffuse treatment read *How Children Think and Learn* (Wood, 1988).

2. Metacognition

Don't get frightened by the word. In simple terms, metacognition means thinking about thinking, so that one has a conscious awareness of it. It correlates with being less impulsive and being more inclined to tackle a task or problem intelligently. If one has a troublesome teenage daughter or son and they are winding you up, you get cross and give them a verbal blast which develops into a row—you have been fairly impulsive. If on the other hand you think for a moment, *'Hm... this is annoying, but I think she is doing this because she needs to establish her identity and independence, so it would probably be better if I...'*, then you are being metacognitive (but you may not be any more successful with your troublesome offspring). If a student, when faced with a geographical issue or problem, asks herself *'What is this about? What have I done before that can help me?'*, then they are using metacognition. Perhaps the best example in this book of students starting to develop this awareness is in the ***Story-telling*** exemplars (see pages 78-96).

One of the keys to developing metacognition with students is developing a language for discussing their thoughts and strategies. Generally as teachers we are not well equipped for this task. Many people are surprised by the level of sophistication students can achieve in thinking about thinking. It is through debriefing that metacognition is developed. For further reading on metacognition, try Brown (1987) and von Wright (1992).

3. Challenge

The short term aim of the strategies in this book is to challenge students, to provide a rich learning environment in which they have to think hard (the term **cognitive conflict** has been used to describe this). This has to be done carefully. There is no point in giving students work which is way beyond their capabilities. As a benchmark, it is educationally healthy to be giving students activities which are just beyond their present capabilities, so that they have to struggle—think how very young children are always trying to do things that are too difficult! The Russian psychologist, Vygotsky, developed the concept of the **zone of proximal development**, which is represented by what a student can do on their own and what they can do supported by more able peers or adults. As teachers we should be trying to move students through their ZPD, helping them to do independently what they can presently do with the assistance of others. There is an excellent example of this in the last ***Odd One Out*** exemplar, where the teacher talks about wiring up the brains of some low achieving students (see page 18).

However, what students can do is highly dependent on their motivation. If they have good self esteem they will tackle most things. It follows therefore that with lower sets one needs to establish a good relationship, in which they trust you and where you are supportive of their efforts and reinforce their successes. This makes an absolutely fantastic difference to what students are prepared to try to do.

As a teacher you can do a great deal for students to help and encourage them to undertake challenging tasks by:

- using explanations, demonstrations, stories and analogies to make sure that that they have an initial purchase on the relevant concepts, skill and language that they need;

- building confidence, and valuing and reinforcing what you see as important in their continued learning (such as listening);
- using the more able students within the class to support the learning of the less able.

A generic term used to describe this process is **scaffolding**.

A final insight into challenge is provided by the concept of transforming. In four of the strategies, students are called upon to transform data from one form to another:

- *Story-telling:* the heard word (from the teacher) is transformed into memory and then back into the spoken word.
- *Living Graphs:* statements are interpreted and transferred (transformed) onto a graph.
- *Mind Movies:* the heard word is transformed into visual images.
- *Reading Photographs:* visual images are transformed into verbal images and relationships.

The very process of transforming requires the brain to process information actively, which in itself provides challenge to the learner.

4. Talk and groupwork

From the above it should be no surprise that **talk** both between students and between students and teachers is fundamental to this approach. It is through language that we achieve much of our learning. There is a phrase *'talking oneself into meaning'*. Almost certainly you have had the experience of talking to someone and they (or you) say *'Now I get it'* or *'I see what you mean'* or *'Do you mean that...?'* Understanding develops through talk as ideas and interpretation are communicated and shared.

Most of these strategies are best employed through **groupwork**. Some research shows that groupwork is not successful as a learning environment, but in these instances it is almost certain that students are doing the same task around a table but with no co-operative learning endeavour (Galton, Simon & Croll, 1985). They are working *in* groups, rather than *as* groups.

Those of you familiar with the National Oracy Project will be aware of the issue of creating a good talk environment (see Carter, 1991). There are some markers that are a useful indication of the quality of talk:

- **reciprocity:** do students respond to and build upon what each other says, or are they like separate radio stations broadcasting on their own wavelength and not receiving? Good talk in groups should be collaborative, as the strengths and weaknesses of different ideas are considered from different perspectives, leading to the acceptance of the better ideas and solutions (Kruger, 1993);
- **speculation, making connections and interpreting:** one report from the National Oracy Project developed these categories of student talk (D'Arcy, 1989), with the suggestion that speculation might be the most highly prized function of talk: *'What if...?'*, *'perhaps...'*, *'I wonder...'*, *'maybe if they...'* are all snippets that we should be pleased to hear;
- **students talking at length:** research from Britain and the US (eg, Sarason, 1982) suggests that in most whole class discussions, the teacher is the main talker, and students rarely get to speak for more than 2 seconds. A question is asked, the student gives a short answer (perhaps one word) and then the teacher finishes off the exchange, almost putting words in their mouths;

- **students initiating:** again depressing evidence abounds to show that there is a consistent pattern to classroom talk. The teacher *initiates*, the student *responds* and the teacher *evaluates* (IRE) (Sinclair & Coulthard, 1975). Students rarely initiate, so these activities are designed to encourage them to do so as they are challenged and begin to speculate;
- **teacher questions:** most teacher questions are closed recall questions: *'What is the climate like in Wales?'*, *'What does condensation mean?'*, *'What is the name of the largest island in Japan?'*, etc. If students are to be encouraged to speculate and feed back their interpretation (construction of meaning) then the teacher needs to ask more open questions. However, closed questions still have their place. These activities encourage the asking of open questions.

There is a great deal of skill in managing groupwork, some of which comes out in the sections on implementing the strategies (see for example Stanford, 1990). Group composition requires some thought, but where possible mixed ability groups are desirable because of the value that variety brings. The less able can be supported by the more able, the more able learn from explaining and interpreting. Furthermore, there are many students who are not brilliant at written work but who are stars in groups and vice versa. Friendship groups have some advantages but they may agree on solutions too easily.

One of the most significant issues in **Thinking Through Geography** activities is when to intervene in a group. It can be very destructive to go up to a group and say *'How are you getting on?'*, as it can break their flow and it may take them a long time to get back to their discussion. There is a tendency for us to feel that we are not doing our job if we are not interacting with students. As a general rule **do not interrupt groups if they are working well, even if this is tempting.** Instead, try to listen to what groups are saying so that you can draw upon their thoughts and insight in the debriefing stage.

For further reading on the importance of small group talk see Sharan (1980) Wood (1980), and Mercer (2000). An excellent general text is *Thinking Voices: the Work of the National Oracy Project* (Norman, 1992). *Importantly,* there is much excellent support material in the KS3 Literacy Strategy relating to talk and group work.

5. Big concepts

We believe that it is helpful to conceive of geography in terms of a number of central underpinning concepts, through which much subject matter is understood. Students find this helpful. Otherwise the subject becomes a mass of rather disconnected content. There is a wonderful quote from a sixth former about science: *'Science was a load of rubbish. One day you would come in and cut up a bull's eye and the next day you would come in and they would tell you what salt was. It was absolute rubbish, it didn't teach you nothing.'* (Ebbutt & Watts, 1987).

Geography is open to the same accusation. Of course we do not claim to have a monopoly of wisdom about the subject, and our list of concepts is open to challenge. We would expect any other gathering of geography teachers to come up with a different list. To a large extent this does not matter—what does matter is that you have a list of concepts that you share with students so that they can understand and use them across a wide variety of contexts. It is our experience that this works extremely well. In Appendix 1, you will find the list of big concepts given some elaboration. The big concepts are made visible through the debriefing.

Our current list is as follows:
- **Cause and effect**
- **Planning**
- **Decision making**
- **Location**
- **Classification**
- **Inequality**
- **Development**
- **Systems**

6. Bridging and transfer

It is the assumed aim of education that what students learn in one context they will be able to **transfer** to and use in another. The evidence is largely to the contrary, hence the comments above by the sixth-former on science. To give a more specific example, the Welsh Board (WJEC) recently carried out an analysis (Battersby, Webster & Younger, 1995) of the Avery Hill (GYSL) GCSE papers and discovered that between 35% and 40% of students score 0 on the case study parts of questions, either through not attempting them or getting no marks. Nearly all the students concerned will have covered one or more case studies (which would have sufficed) and would have remembered something, but they failed to recognise that this is where that knowledge could be used.

In the launching and debriefing sections of some of the exemplars, therefore, we are at pains to give attention to **bridging**. In general terms the teacher encourages the students to see connections between what they have done and learned in this lesson and other contexts. These contexts may be in other units of work in geography, in history, in science or, best of all, in the contexts of their own lives. So, for example, the story about buying a Ford Sierra (see page 56) helps to reinforce the distinction between background and trigger factors. The reference to *Little Red Riding Hood* in the **Story-telling** strategy helps to build a case for remembering through stories. The mention of family disputes over untidy bedrooms provides another context for seeing how viewpoints (and values) influence the interpretation of 'facts'.

If students are successful in using what has been learned in one place, they can be said to have transferred their learning (Blagg, Ballinger & Lewis, 1993). If the context is fairly similar it is termed near transfer, and if the context is very different from the original it is termed far transfer. So if students learn something about decision making in agricultural land use, and use this in another case study it is near transfer. If however they use it in terms of political decisions about limiting greenhouse gas emissions they have achieved far transfer.

Bridging by the teacher may be seen as part of the multiplier factor in taking the learning from an exciting, challenging and enjoyable lesson and making it count in the intellectual development of the student.

For further reading see Perkins & Salomon (1988).

7. Appealing to all the senses

There is a tendency to equate learning with listening (as in lectures and exposition) and reading from textbooks. We feel that it is important to offer students a variety of stimulus formats, so that they can learn by looking (***Reading Photographs***), using their imagination and own experience (***Mind Movies***), talking (***Mysteries***) and listening actively and retelling (***Story-telling***).

For those with an interest in learning styles (see for example Kolb, 1984) or multiple intelligences or accelerated learning, the strategies in this book can be seen as offering fulfilment to a broader range of learning styles than usually occurs. Furthermore, geographical education can make a substantial contribution to visual literacy (see Tufte, 1990 and 1997).

8. Thinking skills plus

Thinking skills approaches do not constitute a whole curriculum in the broadest sense—they are not a complete panacea to all educational ills, however enthusiastic we may be (see graph on page 166).

There are two points we would like to stress in relation to this:

- You may be highly successful in motivating and challenging your students. They become more thoughtful and begin to understand geography through the big concepts which they are start to use in unfamiliar contexts. For some students however, poor literacy may still be a major barrier to achievement, which may seriously handicap them in examinations. The Literacy Strategy at KS3 is an important complement to teaching thinking, as it contains many useful strategies to improve writing.

- Don't forget what you are already good at. Teachers who use thinking skills are not meant to be clones. Effective use may require some changes in classroom practice, but hang on to the things that make you good anyway. This could be good relationships, high expectations, reward systems, setting targets, good display work, using topical events or using drama techniques. These can all happily weld on to the changes implicated here in a productive synergy.

Long term infusion

Using ***Thinking Through Geography*** at level 3 requires planning to go beyond single lessons to consider schemes of work. There are two basic approaches:

1. Putting a number of teaching thinking strategies into each unit of work;
2. Designing a number of units which focus strongly on teaching thinking.

Further guidance is given in *More Thinking Through Geography*.

The National Curriculum and GCSE

It is important that this innovation is not seen as standing outside the formal curriculum that schools have to deliver. You can use the ***Thinking Through Geography*** approach (strategies, materials, and style) and deliver the National Curriculum, GCSE and A Level— and improve results. In effect you go beyond delivering the curriculum by also improving the learning capabilities of your students.

The National Curriculum

Apart from addressing thinking skills, ***Thinking Through Geography*** also helps pupils gain access to higher levels of attainment. Teachers sometimes do not set tasks which allow pupils to show attainment at levels 7 and 8.

The strategies do encourage students to:

- understand interactions within and between physical and human processes (as for example in ***Mysteries, Classification, Story-telling*** and ***Reading Photographs***);

- appreciate the many factors that influence decisions made about places (***Mysteries*** and ***Fact or Opinion***);
- recognise that human actions may have unintended environmental consequences (***Mysteries*** and ***Living Graphs***).

These abilities are crucial to higher achievement.

Secondly, an analysis of the level descriptions shows that students will not be able to advance through the levels just by being taught more content. The levels describe qualitatively different outcomes in terms of students' work. Students need to be taught so that they become more proficient in describing, explaining, evaluating and analysing. Without this, progress through the levels will be painfully slow for many. Being able to describe well is highly dependent on being able to classify; being able to explain is highly dependent on understanding cause and effect; being able to evaluate requires a handle on decision making.

The ***Thinking Through Geography*** Group was responsible for the SCAA Optional Tasks and Tests materials on earthquakes. Like materials in that publication, many of the exemplars in this book have a number of real plusses in relation to NC assessment:

- they tend to be open ended and therefore allow a range of response which can match a spread of levels;
- they are diagnostic—they help in understanding what students are not yet able to do;
- they highlight those important skills that centre on the command verbs such as describe, explain and analyse.

It is too tempting also not to make some comment on OfSTED and inspections. Whilst having many reservations about the criteria and processes that are employed, ***Thinking Through Geography*** materials have come under scrutiny in a number of inspections and have attracted much favourable comment. One of the most common criticisms by OfSTED is that students of middle and high ability are not being challenged. When used well, these materials address that criticism splendidly.

Gifted and Talented, Citizenship and Creativity

Since the first edition of the book, we have become aware that many geography teachers, advisers and trainers have been using ***Thinking Through Geography*** materials for planning provision for gifted and talented pupils and for teaching citizenship. Furthermore, ***Thinking Through Geography*** has much to offer in the area of creativity, which is the subject of development work by QCA.

GCSE

Much of what has been said above applies to GCSE. Doing well in GCSE does not rest heavily on learning pages of notes. Rather it demands that students:

- understand what they have been taught;
- can make sense of the examiation question;
- are able to use the information that is available (data response and stimulus material);
- and can formulate an answer in response to the question posed.

Thinking is a decided advantage here.

If students develop an explicit understanding of the big concepts (or your amended version) they will have a structure around which to build a real understanding of the content that they are taught. If students appreciate the difference between background and trigger causes and factors they are far better placed to deal with GCSE exams. Finally, most exam Boards offer a syllabus with a decision making paper and *Thinking Through Geography* is an apprenticeship in such exercises.

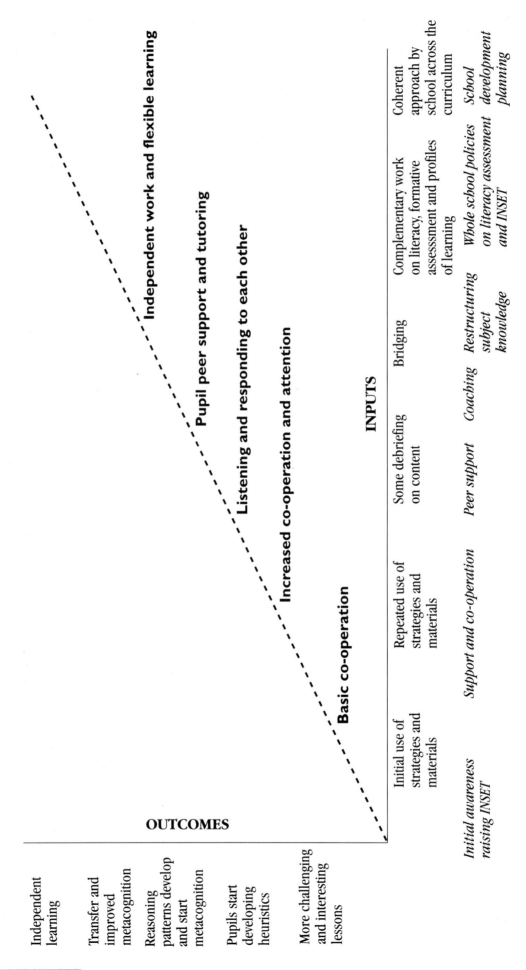

Appendix 1: Big concepts

We have some reticence in presenting this list. It is not a definitive list, and many other alternative lists could be generated. It is meant to be a dynamic framework—to be added to and subtracted from with time. It is generated largely from our understanding of what students find useful in coming to understand the topics that the National Curriculum, GCSE and A Level syllabuses present. Remember the main concern in this book is students' learning, not the sanctity of the subject. In some cases our understanding has been generated from things that students have said—their understanding. These concepts are organic, they grow with the students and they greatly assist in the transfer of learning. At the end of each description are three or four principle tenets relating to the concept, which seem to aid student understanding. They are not taught directly, but they can be developed through the use of the *Thinking Through Geography* materials and their debriefing. Herein lies the nub of the new teaching skill that needs to be developed. It is freely admitted that in some concepts our thoughts are more developed than in others. We hope that you and your students will add to both the number and the depth of these tenets.

Cause and effect

Almost every time students are asked to explain, give reasons, account for and do 'Why?' questions they are calling upon their understanding of causation. We tend to be satisfied if lower achieving students give a few reasons, but there is so much more to causation that students can be brought to understand.

The NC level descriptors require an understanding of causation. For example Level 5 includes the following:

> *'Pupils... describe and begin to offer explanations for geographical patterns and for a range of physical and human processes.... They offer explanations for ways in which human activities affect the environment.'*

To move towards Level 8 the challenge to teachers is not to cover more content, but to bring about a qualitative change in students' thinking and writing. The description is as follows:

> *'They offer explanations for interactions within and between physical and human processes. They explain changes over time in the characteristics of places.... Pupils recognise the causes and consequences of environmental issues and show understanding of different approaches to tackling them.'*

These level statements are so much more attainable if the concepts of cause and effect are deliberately developed. All students have access to a great deal of personal experience of causation—things happen to them, their families and their friends every day.

Cause

The causation of events can be understood through what we have come to call **trigger** and **background** factors. Background factors are those which predispose events to happen. They tend to be permanent and more abstract, widespread and endemic. They will often be the physical, economic, social and political factors that we are accustomed to referring to. Trigger factors are more episodic, visible and localised, which make something happen to a particular person, on a particular day, in a particular place. A good analogy is the match (trigger) that starts a fire in a tinder dry forest after a long period of drought (background). Of course some factors seem to fall between the two, so perhaps causative factors are a continuum rather than two separate groups. The more able students can understand and include background factors more successfully in their explanations, because they can deal with abstract thinking. The less able students tend to focus on the more visible trigger factors. Explanation can usefully be structured to start with trigger factors and then proceed to the background, or vice versa, but an unsorted jumble of factors will be less coherent. Insights into trigger and background factors are well developed through *Mysteries*.

However, much geography is not rooted in events; it is to do with patterns and trends—the growth of out-of-town shopping centres, migration, the rise of Mediterranean resorts, the shrinking of the polar ice caps, and the increase in human intervention in drainage basins. Thus background factors are the dominant mode of explanation, making understanding and success so difficult for less able students. Introducing people is extremely helpful, as is demonstrated in *Living Graphs,* as it makes causation less abstract.

Another attribute of successful explanation is grouping of causes. *Mysteries* encourage students to group information in the very physical sense that pieces of paper are arranged together. Again this is actively encouraged in *Mysteries* and to some extent in the *Classification* exemplars.

Linkage is a key attribute of good causal explanation, one point should lead to another. This is clearly demonstrated and developed in the *Story-telling* exemplars which use story-boarding.

Effect

Effects can be actual (they have happened) or future (they may happen in the future. Speculating coherently about the future is a demanding cognitive activity, because it requires the checking of assumptions and the assessment of likelihood.

Effects can be short, medium or long term. The short term effects are likely to be more localised and visible and relate directly to a visible population (victims of a disaster). Long term effects are more diffuse, abstract and enduring. Future, projected effects can be rated as probable, possible or unlikely. Effects can be strong or weak, depending on the magnitude of impact. Effects can be widespread, affecting a large number of people or large area, or localised, affecting a small area or particular group of people.

The Kanto earthquake exemplar (*Classification*) and the *Nuclear disaster* **Mind Movie** are two examples where a generic understanding of the concept of effect can be developed.

Systems

Whole volumes have been written about systems, and although they are no longer headline news, they are probably greatly underdeveloped as a tool. There is a strong overlap with cause and effect because change can be understood partly by reference to change in inputs, affecting structures and processes, leading to change in outputs or effects. Cities, farms, landscapes, biomes, factories, the atmosphere, communities, sand dunes, and populations can all be represented as systems.

In thinking of KS3 and KS4, there are a few principles which students can usefully develop which have great power:

- most systems (open systems) have inputs and outputs, structures and processes;
- systems have structures and processes which are adapted to environmental conditions. If inputs change, there will consequential change in the system's structures and processes. So towns change if there is an increased input in terms of traffic or population. These can be termed feedback loops;
- systems reach a harmony or equilibrium, where inputs are stable.

Systems are not too well represented in the exemplars. *The lost animals of Loxley Coppice Farm* **Mystery** offers some reinforcement of systems, but as it is an A Level activity it does not make a good starting place.

Classification

This is an unfamiliar concept to geographers, but it is regarded as central in science. Classification is crucial to processing information and ultimately to the process of describing. We do not deal with every perceptual input as new and discrete information, we tend to classify it by looking at the attributes, but each phenomenon usually has a range of attributes. A particular motor vehicle may be green, a hatchback, a Ford, have four wheels, be rusty and have a Newcastle United sticker in the back. To most people the most important attribute is the four wheels and we just register it as a car. However, certain individuals may particularly notice the rust or the sticker and go further in classifying the car and therefore in responding to and thinking about the car.

- Classifications are hierarchical. Categories can be merged and split. Ford motor cars can be split on colour or model. The categories in the *Classification* exemplars can be further split or merged.
- Categories used in a classification or the assignment of a phenomenon to a category depend on the purpose one has. The purpose determines which characteristic or trait to select as the super-ordinate characteristic, and this is often heavily influenced by values. Thus the North Sea may be seen as a place to fish, a recreational resource, water to cross, a major ecological resource, or a dumping ground by (respectively) a trawler skipper, a windsurfer, a ferry company executive, a marine ecologist or a sewage engineer.
- Thus values or perspectives are important in determining which attribute is most influential in the process of classifying. One needs to check the basis from which one classifies.

Classification underpins many of the activities in this book, ie, *Classification, Odd One Out, Mysteries,* and *Fact or Opinion. Fact or Opinion*, in particular, brings out the crucial relationship between values and classification.

Location

Location keeps cropping up in geography, but it gets very little explicit attention except in industrial location, where we keep peddling the same outdated 1960s determinism. An understanding of the concept of location can span a number of topics which are not normally associated—industrial location, retailing distribution patterns, ecological succession, the geography of health (both distribution of services and outbreaks of disease), crime patterns, and tourist development.

- **Resource or concentrated location.** Some economic, natural and human activities are sensibly located near the resource that they require. This applies as much to some forms of recreation (paragliding and surfing) and oceanic biomass (fish near upwelling cold currents) as it does to industrial location (timber mills and sugar beet factories). Admittedly the reasons are somewhat different.
- **Dispersed locations.** Some activities are more evenly spread. Thus schools are located largely to serve the population and are located in proportion to population. People usually spread themselves out fairly evenly on a beach in order to gain a reasonable share of the space. Many plants which compete for water or light will be fairly evenly distributed. However it has to be recognised that dispersed locations can be a subset of concentrated locations. In the case of the beach, given above, sunbathers are concentrated on beaches by the sea, where they then spread themselves out.
- **Mutual attraction location.** Many human activities are drawn together, because they provide reciprocal advantage in being located together.
- Friction of distance and intervening opportunity often distort the patterns that would result in the above.

Unfortunately there are no activities that relate strongly to location in this book.

Planning

There is more to planning than land use regulation systems with which we tend to associate the word. Planning is a fundamental human activity engaged in by both individuals and societies. Planning is therefore of underpinning importance in a range of geographic spheres—urban and economic geography, tourism, hazard management, and development issues.

- Planning is about wholes and parts. Plans have to have details which meet some of the requirements of the brief, but they also need to make a coherent whole in which the parts fit together.
- Planning depends upon predicting the future, because it is meeting the needs of the future that inspires the human urge to plan. This is done both through careful data collection to describe the present, and through projection and imagination, creating visions of expected and desirable futures.
- Planning is done both by the individual and by authorities. Individuals plan for themselves and for the short and medium term. Authorities plan on a bigger scale for the short and medium term, and sometimes for the long term.
- Planning has to take account of the present. Whatever is planned for the future, it has to be grafted on to what already exists. This is as true for putting an extension on a house as it is for planning flood relief schemes for a large city.

Decision making

Decision making has one of the most visible places in geography because of the increasing popularity of decision making papers at A Level and GCSE. It is difficult to understand the people environment relationship without an appreciation of decision making processes. The more explicit this understanding is, the more it can be applied to curricular decision making scenarios. It also provides an appreciable insight into the comparison of cultures and values in education generally.

- Decision making is based on values and perspectives, which predispose certain standpoints. These are used to evaluate information or to confirm a decision. This is well illustrated in the ***Fact or Opinion*** exemplars.
- Decision making is heavily influenced by images and experience. Of course these have been influenced by attitudes, because they affect the processing of information.
- Collective decision making is determined by power. Some individuals and groups have a great deal of power, which they exercise with varying degrees of autocracy. Some groups have little power and are likely to lose out as a result of decision making. This is evident in the *Sharpe Point **Mystery***.
- Decision making creates conflict which can be resolved by a variety of recognisable methods:

(i) *Brute force:* those in power may simply impose their will and 'take all'. (Some miners, logging companies and hydro companies have used brute force against South American Indians.)

(ii) *Amelioration (sweetening the pill):* whatever the adverse effects the decision makers try to reduce the effects on the losers. (Householders living near the new road may get landscaping and double glazing.)

(iii) *Zoning:* it is possible that certain areas in the decision making area will be allocated to one interest group and others to competing interests. (On Lake District lakes certain areas allow power boats, others cater for sailing boats and canoes and some areas are for the birds alone.)

(iv) *Time solutions:* one user may get priority use at one time of day, week or year, while another user takes over at other times. (Fishing seasons allow anglers to use rivers during certain months, canoeists will be allowed during some months and during the spawning season the fish have the river to themselves.)

(v) *Replacement:* if something is destroyed the winners may replace with a replica elsewhere. (If a housing development destroys a flower rich meadow, the turf may be removed or another meadow created elsewhere.)

(vi) *Buying off:* the losers in a decision may be given money or some other compensation to remove their objections. (Farmers whose land will be flooded by a new reservoir will have land bought by compulsory purchase.)

Inequality

In science, compensation and equilibrium is a key concept because it helps to explain much of what happens in the physical world. However this applies equally to geography. Migration is caused by inequality, either real or perceived, which can relate to economic difference or freedom/oppression. Crime can be partly attributed to inequalities, and is certainly related to changes in employment. Winds blow because of inequalities in pressure. Rivers flow because of inequalities in energy. If land rises rivers downcut in an effort to achieve a new equilibrium. Much is made of industries competing on a level playing field.

- Compensating movements of, for example, people, water and energy, will tend to even out inequalities.
- Friction tends to reduce this tendency and acts as a force for inertia. People often do not migrate because of family and emotional ties or a fear of the new. Landslides may be delayed because of friction. Firms may not relocate because of industrial inertia.
- Restraining forces, put in place by people, also act to counter compensatory movements. In China, there are restrictions on migration to prevent an urbanisation explosion. Engineering works are used to help prevent sudden mass movements such as landslides. Traffic management is used in some areas of national parks to prevent overuse of fragile areas and congestion on the roads.

Development

Much debate continues over interpretations of development, but we find it useful to see it in terms of quality of life for individuals and communities. Of course such a term is equally fraught, but useful insight can be developed whilst allowing for debate. To allow for debate (and our uncertainty) three of the points below are presented as questions.

- Quality of life can be related to human rights. To what extent do people have a right to: food and water, jobs, education, medical care, homes, democracy, freedom of speech, freedom from oppression? Which of these are most important?
- Is quality of life relative to culture? Are all the measures above pertinent to all cultures? Should Islamic or aboriginal cultures be judged by the same standards as a Western culture?
- To what extent can and should factors such as happiness, harmony, equality, social cohesion and spirituality be used in judging quality of life?
- Development may be judged in terms of its ecological and social sustainability.

Although the exemplars on the *Los Angeles riots* and the *Stage model of tourism* were not steered in this direction, they are suitable for developing insights into development, through the debriefing process.

* * * * * *

This book was not written so that all these concepts were elaborated by the strategies. It was written to encourage teachers to start using challenging strategies.

We hope that this 'Cook's tour' of our view of important concepts will give a stimulus to those who wish to make a start on rebuilding their geography curriculum, using these strategies as a building block.

Appendix 2:
Professional Development

There have been several references in the book to the importance of professional development as a necessary condition to make these strategies work well. You may have found difficulties yourself or have experienced difficulties in getting colleagues to use them. It needs to be recognised that change in classroom practice is achieved only at some emotional cost (Leat, 1993; Rich, 1993). Adopting innovative practices has the effect of turning experts back into relative novices. There is often a dip in confidence and a feeling of being deskilled, because one's routines are overturned. The classroom becomes unpredictable. It is depressing to reflect that many good innovations have failed, because teachers were not supported adequately to bring about necessary changes. A number of writers have reached the conclusion that—*"There is no curriculum development without teacher development"*.

Much of the work by Newcastle University's Thinking Skills Research Group since the first edition of this book has been focused on learning to help teachers and schools implement teaching thinking successfully. The article (Leat, 1999) *Rolling the Stone Uphill* outlines the common barriers, experienced by teachers in implementation:

- The socialising effect of schools on teachers and pupils which stimulate both teachers and pupils to conform to traditional, 'normal' behaviour patterns.
- The routine behaviours or craft knowledge that one develops to make lessons run smoothly are often not sufficient to make teaching thinking work well. For example questioning may need to change from mainly closed questions to mainly open questions—a difficult shift.
- Teachers tend to know their subject in the form of the content presented in schemes of work, syllabuses and the double page spreads of text books. Often they are unfamiliar with the underlying structure of the subject—for example the 'big' concepts.
- We all have beliefs about teaching and for some teachers they do not match the principles or practice of teaching thinking. An example might be a belief that pupils have to have written work in their books otherwise they have done no 'work'.

The Research Group has worked with a number of school and LEA networks—the North East School-Based Research Consortium (funded by the Teacher Training Agency) and the Northumberland Humanities Network. Through interviews, field notes, teachers' diary entries and in-service session discussions a number of important principles have emerged:

- Teachers need to experiment in their classrooms and they need to feel safe in experimenting. New knowledge cannot just be given to teachers. It is only understood through use. This has been termed 'tinkering'. But this tinkering should be structured in a way that helps the teacher learn from the process and avoid wasting energy on fruitless experiments.
- The power of networks, both within and beyond the school. The benefits of such networks are incalculable but some of the most important benefits are practical advice, emotional support, shared language, enhanced motivation and exchange of ideas and resources. Networks sustain people.
- Coaching teachers in teaching thinking works impressively. Once coaches have been trained, cross-subject coaching appears to be more successful than within subject coaching. Within subject coaching would probably work better across schools.
- With or without coaching, teachers recording their lessons on video and using them for reflective enquiry and analysis leads to profound professional learning.
- The support and active involvement of school senior managers is paramount in making teaching thinking work from Level 2 upwards.
- Individual and networks of teachers need to be connected to outside agencies such as higher education, advisers and school improvement projects who can connect them to research and ideas that can move their thinking and practice on.
- A focus on teaching thinking should not be regarded as another initiative. Meaningful school improvement is achieved by focusing on the quality of classroom teaching and learning. Teaching

thinking can substantially deliver on improving literacy, citizenship, disaffection and motivation, learning styles, raising attainment, key skills and improving professional development. You just need some connected thinking.

Professional learning communities

The Times Educational Supplement carried a front page headline in July 2001 about young teachers fleeing the profession feeling that they were being bullied by senior managers to meet targets, without necessary support. If this is a fair reflection then it points to the absolute necessity of changing tack and turning schools into **professional learning communities.**

'Learning and Teaching—A strategy for professional development' (DfEE, 2001) highlights the fact that teachers want to learn 'on the job'. It records that when teachers are asked about activities that have most impact on their classroom practice they mainly mention two things:

1. Learning with and from other teachers, in their own or other schools by:
   - Observing other colleagues teaching and discussing the lesson;
   - Collaborative enquiry into school improvement problems;
   - Taking part in coaching or mentoring.
2. High quality focused training on specific skill areas, underpinned by excellent teaching materials and direct support to apply their learning back in the classroom.

It is further highlighted that among the circumstances that lead to successful changes in teachers' practice are:
- Opportunities for teachers to reflect;
- Opportunities to understand the rationale behind new ideas;
- Sustained opportunities to experiment with new ideas and approaches;
- Support from headteachers and heads of department and participation in wider teacher networks.

This is a model that fits our experience of what makes teaching thinking work well. It should be welcomed.

Classroom Observation

One of the important changes in professional development that one would expect to see is a change in approaches to classroom observation. With the introduction of performance management, more lessons are being observed by senior teachers. The common outcome from this is that a judgement is made about the lesson, perhaps with some feedback about possible improvements. Relatively few teachers report that this process is helping to improve their practice.

Table 1 opposite provides the basis for an observation schedule for teaching thinking lessons. This schedule, or one adapted from it, could be given to a senior manager who was going to observe a lesson, which gives much greater control over the process to the teacher. It could have the effect of beginning to get senior management involvement and engagement. It could be used in an observation by a coach or in observing a more experienced teacher, or even in watching a video of oneself.

One might summarise this approach to change as bottom-up change supported from the top. Michael Fullan's excellent book *Change Forces—The Sequel,* presents a fuller view of change management.

Some of the implications are represented in the graph on page 166. The graph suggests that there may be different levels of outcome from thinking skills lessons. To achieve these, professional practice has to develop through certain levels or barriers which requires insight, motivation and resources. The graph has the disadvantage of suggesting that there is a simple relationship between teacher development and outcomes—clearly it is not as straightforward as this. The graph is there to communicate an idea about the importance of professional development.

A further model is shown in **Figure 1** *(page 174)*. This model has been adapted from a report on effective teachers of numeracy (Askew *et al.* 1997), but we believe that it has wider salience. The model was developed to explain how the most effective teachers become effective. It is through the interaction of their beliefs, their knowledge for teaching, their classroom practices and pupils' response. The space between the inner and outer circles in the model represents the zone of interaction and change. One can map possible uses of this book and its approach onto that model. It will be assumed first that your beliefs about teaching are in general

One of the important changes in professional development that one would expect to see is a change in approaches to classroom observation. With the introduction of performance management, more lessons are being observed by senior teachers. The common outcome from this is that a judgement is made about the lesson, perhaps with some feedback about possible improvements. Relatively few teachers report that this process is helping to improve their practice.

This schedule, or one adapted from it, could be given to a senior manager who was going to observe a lesson, which gives much greater control over the process to the teacher. It could have the effect of beginning to get senior management involvement and engagement. It could be used in an observation by a coach or in observing a more experienced teacher, or even in watching a video of oneself.

One might summarise this approach to change as bottom-up change supported from the top. Michael Fullan's excellent book *Change Forces—The Sequel,* presents a fuller view of change management.

Some of the implications are represented in the graph on page 166. The graph suggests that there may be different levels of outcome from thinking skills lessons. To achieve these, professional practice has to develop through certain levels or barriers which requires insight, motivation and resources. The graph has the disadvantage of suggesting that there is a simple relationship between teacher development and outcomes—clearly it is not as straightforward as this. The graph is there to communicate an idea about the importance of professional development.

A further model is shown in **Figure 1** *(page 174)*. This model has been adapted from a report on effective teachers of numeracy (Askew *et al.* 1997), but we believe that it has wider salience. The model was developed to explain how the most effective teachers become effective. It is through the interaction of their beliefs, their knowledge for teaching, their classroom practices and pupils' response. The space between the inner and outer circles in the model represents the zone of interaction and change. One can map possible uses of this book and its approach onto that model. It will be assumed first that your beliefs about teaching are in general alignment with teaching thinking. One could categorise the book as 'knowledge of approaches' which will impact positively on your knowledge for planning and perhaps reinforce your beliefs. You plan to use some of the material in the classroom and you adjust some aspects of your practice, by perhaps allowing pupils to struggle intellectually with an open task and not giving detailed instructions about how to do it. The pupils really get into it and enjoy both the task and giving their ideas. Their response is positive therefore and this feedback effects on your practice, knowledge for planning and beliefs. However your attempts at asking pupils about how they have done the task meet with blank looks and silence. This may discourage that part of your attempts to change your practice. To provide a contrast, consider a teacher who by virtue of their beliefs is less open and sympathetic to teaching thinking. Their knowledge for planning and their planning does not change. They introduce a mystery without much thought or attention, the pupils are confused by the unfamiliar demands and some mess around. The feedback to this teacher is negative and there is no impetus or energy that could drive the development of their thinking or practice, the attempt to change will peter out and the status quo will resume.

The importance of the model is that coaching, collaboration and networks can make the arrows work. The arrows represent meaningful professional development to make the classroom a more challenging and effective learning environment. Coaching, collaboration and networks mean that there is emotional support, good advice, 'sparky' ideas, precise feedback and some fun. All of which needs to take place in a school atmosphere that is supportive of developing practice, taking sensible risks in the classroom and enquiry into teaching and learning. Schools should concern themselves with learning.

Fig. 1 A model to explain development of effective practice (after Askew et al., 1997).

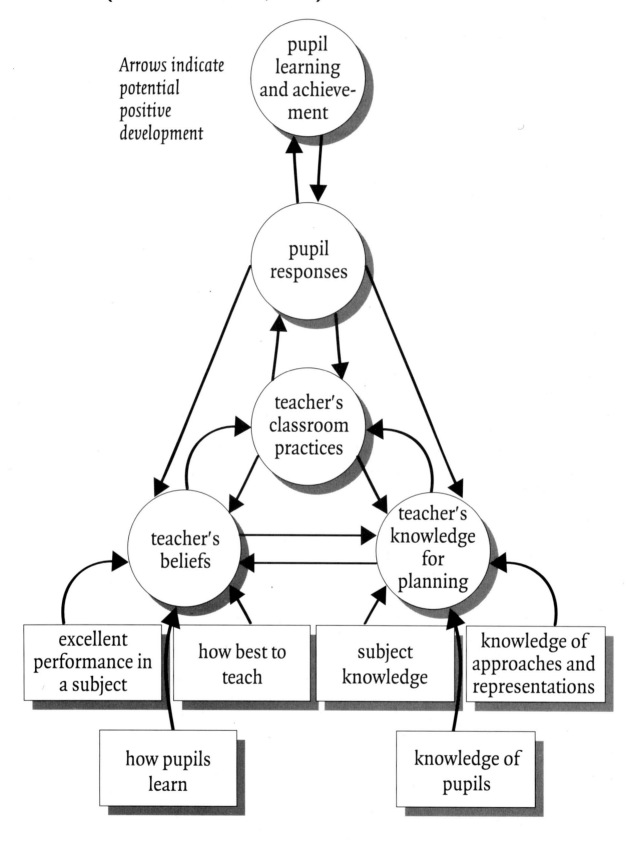

References

Adey, P. & Shayer, M. (1994) *Really Raising Standards*, London: Routledge.

Askew, M., Brown, M., Rhodes, V., Johnson, D. & Wiliam, D. (1997) *Effective Teachers of Numeracy—Final Report*, London: King's College, London.

Battersby, J., Webster, A. & Younger, M. (1995) *The Case Study in GCSE Geography: Experiences from the Avery Hill Project*, Cardiff: Welsh Joint Education Committee.

Blagg, N., Ballinger, M. & Lewis, R. (1993) Development of transferable skills in learners, *R & D Series No. 18*, Cambridge: Employment Department.

Brown, A. L. (1987) Metacognition, executive control, self regulation and other more mysterious mechanisms, in Weinert, Franz, Kluwe & Rainer (eds) *Metacognition, Motivation and Understanding*, London: Lawrence Erlbaum Associates.

Carter, R. (ed.) (1991) *Talking About Geography*, Sheffield: Geographical Association

Costa, A. & Garmston, R. (1994) *Cognitive Coaching: A Foundation for Renaissance Schools*, Norwood, Massachusetts: Christopher-Gordon Publishers.

Counsell, C. (1997) *Analytical and Discursive Writing at Key Stage 3*, London: Historical Association.

D'Arcy, P. (1989) *Oracy in Action: A Video-Based Training Package on Oracy in Secondary Schools*, Swindon: Wiltshire LEA.

Department for Education and Employment/Qualifications and Curriculum Authority (1999) *The National Curriculum—Handbook for secondary teachers in England Key Stages 3 and 4*, London, DfEE/QCA.

Driver, R., Squires, A., Rushworth, P. & Wood-Robinson, V. (1994) *Making Sense of Secondary Science*, London: Routledge.

Dweck, C. (2000) *Self-Theories: Their Role in Motivation Personality and Development*, Philadelphia, Pennsylvania: Psychology Press.

Ebbutt, D. & Watts, M. (1987) *Science is Like a Spider's Web: Some sixth formers' views of their science education 11–16*, London: Secondary Science Curriculum Review.

Fullan, M. (1999) *Change Forces: The Sequel*, London: Falmer Press.

Galton, M., Simon, R. & Croll, P. (1985) *Inside the Primary Classroom*, London: Routledge, Kegan & Paul.

Huberman, M. (2000) Networks that alter teaching: conceptualisations, exchanges and experiments, in J. Soler, A. Craft and H. Burgess (eds) *Teacher Development—Exploring Our Own Practice*, London: Paul Chapman Publishing in association with the Open University Press.

Kolb, D. (1984) *Experiential Learning*, New Jersey: Prentice Hall.

Kruger, A.C. (1993) Peer collaboration: conflict, co-operation or both? *Social Development*, Vol. 2, pp 165-182.

Leat, D. (1999) Rolling the Stone Uphill: teacher development and implementation of Thinking Skills programmes, *Oxford Review of Education*, Vol. 25, pp. 387-403.

Leat, D. & Kinninment, D. (2000) Learn to Debrief, in C. Fisher & T. Binns (eds) *Issues in Geography Teaching*, London: RoutledgeFalmer.

Lewis, M. & Wray, D. (1995) *Writing Frames: Scaffolding children's non-fiction writing in a range of genres*, Reading: University of Reading.

Light, P. & Butterworth, G. (eds.) (1992) *Context and Cognition: Ways of Learning and Knowing*, London: Harvester Wheatsheaf.

McGuinness, C. (1999) *From Thinking Skills to Thinking Classrooms: a review and evaluation of approaches for developing pupils' thinking*. DfEE Research Report RR115, London: DfEE.

Mercer, N. (2000) *Words and minds: how we use language to think together*, London: Routledge.

Nichols, A. & Kinninment, D. (2001) *More Thinking Through Geography*, Cambridge: Chris Kington Publishing.

Norman, K. (ed.) (1992) *Thinking Voices: The Work of the National Oracy Project*, London: Hodder and Stoughton.

Perkins, D. & Salomon, G. (1988) Teaching for Transfer, *Educational Leadership*, Vol. 46, pp 22-32.

Sharan, S. (1980) Co-operative Learning in Small Groups: Recent methods and effects on achievement, attitudes and ethnic relations, *Review of Educational Research*, Vol. 50, pp 241-247.

Sinclair, J. & Coulthard, M. (1975) *Towards an Analysis of Discourse: the Language of Teachers and Pupils*, London: Oxford University Press.

Stanford, G. (1990) *Developing Effective Classroom Groups*, Bristol: Acora Books.

Tufte, E. (1990) *Envisioning Information*, Cheshire, Connecticut: Graphics Press.

Tufte, E. (1997) *Visual Explanations, Images and Quantities, Evidence and Narrative*, Cheshire, Connecticut: Graphics Press.

von Wright, J. (1992) Reflections on Learning, *Learning and Instruction*, Vol. 2, pp 59-68.

Wood, D. (1980) Teaching the Young Child: Some relationships between social interaction, language and thought, in D. Olson (ed.) *The Social Foundations of Language and Thought*, New York: Norton.

Wood, D. (1988) *How Children Think and Learn*, Oxford: Blackwell.

Further useful reading:

Baron, J.B. & Sternberg, R.J. (1987) *Teaching Thinking Skills: Theory and Practice*, New York: Freeman.

Burden, R. & Williams, M. (eds.) (1998) *Thinking Through the Curriculum*, London: Routledge.

Maclure, S. & Davies, P. (1991) *Learning to Think: Thinking to Learn—The Proceedings of the 1989 OECD Conference*, Oxford: Pergamon Press.

Nickerson, R.S., Perkins, D.N. & Smith, E.E. (1985) *The Teaching of Thinking*, New Jersey: Lawrence Erlbaum Associates.

Novak, J. D. & Gowin, D. B. (1984) *Learning How to Learn*, Cambridge: CUP.

Resnick, L.B. (1987) *Education and Learning to Think*, Washington: National Academy Press.

Slater, F. (1989) *Language and Learning in the Teaching of Geography*, London: Routledge.